TRUST GOD
FOR
YOUR FINANCES

Brother Bob Fess –

I pray that the Lord
will lead you to help
me distribute this book.
Please pray about this.
Thank you and God bless
you.

Your brother
in Christ,

Jack Hartman

Jack Hartman

9/9/84

Library of Congress Catalog Card Number 83-051358

*"The Lord gave the word:
great was the company
of those that published it."*
Psalm 68:11

First printing - 11/83 - 20,000 copies
Second printing - 7/84 -20,000 copies

Published by:

WORD ASSOCIATES

P.O. Box 3293   Manchester, NH 03105

Printed by Custom Graphics, Tulsa, Oklahoma

Contents

Introduction

I have written this book to help people escape from financial problems. Tens of millions of people suffer from financial problems and they don't know how to escape. I know how these people feel because I also have suffered from very severe financial problems.

I'm a self-employed businessman. Approximately ten years ago our business ran into significant financial problems and I soon found myself with total business debts of approximately ten times my annual income. These debts had grown so rapidly that I found my annual debt repayment schedule was considerably more than my annual income!

For many months I was on the edge of a nervous breakdown. I had a lot of trouble sleeping and I worried almost constantly. My thoughts were consumed with fear of losing my business, fear of losing our home and concern with what my family would think of me for putting them through all of these problems.

Everyone whom I turned to for advice told me that there was only one way out—to file bankruptcy. I refused to believe that this was the only solution. Deep down inside of myself I knew that there had to be a better solution.

At that time, a friend of mine convinced me of my need to accept Jesus Christ as my Lord and Saviour. He also told me that I didn't have to file bankruptcy. He said that there were other answers to my problems and that I could find these answers in the Bible He told me that *every* word in the Bible is inspired by God Himself. "*All* scripture is given by inspiration of God . . ." II Timothy 3:16).

My friend told me that I needed to "saturate" myself in the Bible—to study and meditate in it day and night. This is exactly what I did. For several months I spent tremendous amounts of time studying and meditating on everything that I found in the Bible that even remotely explained how to solve financial problems.

I applied each of these Biblical principles to my financial problems and they worked! This took some time, but the finances of our business turned around and we are now doing very well. The debts have been repaid and, in spite of the economy, we are now in our eighth consecutive year of solid growth over the preceding year!

After studying the Bible by myself for almost a year and a half, I started to meet each Tuesday night with three other businessmen who came to our office to study the Bible. At first this was just a general discussion, but after a few weeks I started preparing and teaching these Bible studies. They grew so rapidly that we had to move on four different occasions in order to accomodate the crowds which have been as large as 300 people.

These Tuesday night Bible studies have now grown into a church with two full-time pastors, a full-time assistant pastor, a large administrative staff and an average Sunday morning attendance of between 900 and 1000 people. I take absolutely no credit for this. The Lord merely used me at the start. Others have had much more to do with this growth than I have.

The important thing to point out is that the growth of our business and the growth of our church have come as a result of applying the Biblical principles that are explained in this book. Many seemingly impossible obstacles have been overcome because God's laws will always overcome the world's obstacles to the exact degree that we know these laws, believe them in our hearts, apply them in our lives and stick to them with unwavering faith.

The principles in this book are not theoretical. They have worked in my life. I have seen them work in the lives of my business associates and in the lives of many of my friends throughout this country and, in fact, around the world. I have seen them work in our church and in the lives of many members of our church.

They have worked for all of these people and they will work for you—the reader of this book. God has no favorites. What He does for one, He will do for others — ". . . God is no respecter of persons" (Acts 10:34). However, we must do our part and our part involves a lot of study and meditation and hard work—"Study to shew thyself approved unto God, a workman that needeth not to be ashamed, rightly dividing the word of truth" (II Timothy 2:15).

I urge you to approach this book with an "I've got to see the answer in the Scriptures before I believe it" attitude. Every point that I make in this book will be backed up by scripture. This book won't contain a few verses of scripture that I can use as a basis for my pet theories. Instead, you will find that this book is actually saturated with dozens of verses of scripture. My theories are *not* important. The important thing is what God's Word says and my *only* function is to explain and to correlate the various verses of scripture from God's Word.

You can place your faith in these financial principles. If we can't believe God's promises in the area of our finances, *how* can we be sure that we can believe His promises for our eternal salvation? If we can believe *some* of what God's Word says, we should be able to believe *all* that God's Word says!

My greatest desire in life is to communicate the teachings of God's Word to other people. Join with me and let's study together exactly what the Scriptures teach us about how we can trust God for our finances.

Chapter One

Should Christians Prosper?

Have you ever asked yourself any of the following questions?

"Does God really want me to be financially prosperous? Doesn't the Bible say that money is the root of all evil?"

"Does God really care about my financial condition?"

"Does God care if I drive an old car and live in a rundown apartment or if I drive a Mercedes and live in a $200,000 home?"

"Won't I prosper if I just work hard?"

"Does the Bible teach us to get out of debt?"

"Is tithing for today?"

"How can I possibly increase my giving if I can't even pay my bills with the money that I earn now?"

"Is it wrong for Christians to have substantial amounts of money in bank accounts and investments?"

Each of these questions and many similar questions will be answered in this book. First of all, we must start with the two extreme positions which Chrisians take today concerning the area of finances.

One extreme concerns those people who hear some of God's laws of prosperity and they say, "This is exactly what I've been looking for. I want a lot of nice things. I'm going to try these laws to see if they work because I need more money, I need a nice car and I want a nicer home."

This approach is wrong. It has too many "I's" in it. This is the *world's* approach to prosperity. We can't "bend" God's laws to fit our selfish desires. We can't "believe for riches" just for the sake of riches. In this book, we'll explain in detail why God's Word says that the world's "me first" system of prosperity is wrong.

However, before we get into this, we first of all have to discuss the opposite extreme—the belief that financial prosperity for Christians is totally wrong. Tens of millions of Christians believe that poverty is godly. They believe that financial prosperity destroys humility and that this lack of humility will draw us away from God.

This and all other objections to financial prosperity are really objections to the *world's* system of financial prosperity. There is no question that the Bible warns us again and again against prospering in this manner.

However, there is another way to prosper and this is by following God's laws of prosperity which are outlined in His Word. If we follow these laws exactly, we'll prosper exactly the way that God wants us to prosper and there is absolutely *nothing* wrong with this kind of prosperity.

Many Christians believe that "money is the root of all evil." This is incorrect. Money by itself is not evil. Money builds churches. Money sends missionaries all over the world. Money produces Christian

14

radio and television programs. Money produces Christian books and cassette tapes.

No, money is not evil. The Bible actually tells us, "For the love of money is the root of all evil: which while some coveted after, they have erred from the faith, and pierced themselves through with many sorrows" (I Timothy 6:10).

Loving money is evil. Putting money first—ahead of God in any way—is evil. Covetousness is evil and a covetous attitude is against the teachings of God's Word and will bring many sorrows into our lives just as the Bible says that it will.

However, there is a way to prosper that is not evil and that is to follow God's laws of prosperity. When this is done, we will prosper financially and we will also prosper physically, mentally and emotionally. This is exactly what our Father in heaven wants for us.

God created all the wealth of this earth. Did He create it for unbelievers—for hard hearted, sinful men and women who curse Him, deny Him and disobey His laws? Does He really want them to prosper and His children to do without? This doesn't make any sense at all. God is no different from any other father. He wants the best for His children.

Our Father doesn't want us to be financial failures in any way. Just as children in the world are a reflection of their parents, Christians should be a reflection of God. He wants the world to see prosperous, joyful, loving Christians. These Christians are a great witness to the world.

If our Father was willing to give us His only Son, why then would He hold anything else back from us??? He has already given us His best. Does

15

it make any sense to believe He would refuse to give us the rest? "He that spared not his own Son, but delivered him up for us all, how shall he not with him also freely give us all things?" (Romans 8:32).

Many great men of God have prospered as a result of following God's laws of prosperity. One good example of the application of these laws can be seen in the life of Abraham. Abraham lived a very fruitful, prosperous life. "And Abram was very rich in cattle, in silver, and in gold" (Genesis 13:2).

The New Testament clearly teaches that, because of the price paid by Jesus Christ, all Christians are heirs to these same blessings that Abraham received from God. "That the blessing of Abraham might come on the Gentiles through Jesus Christ . . ." (Galatians 3:14). "And if ye be Christ's, then are ye Abraham's seed, and heirs according to the promise" (Galatians 3:29).

God's Word clearly tells us that we are heirs to Abraham. This means that the blessings God gave to Abraham are available to us. Our Father wants us to receive the same blessings that He gave to Abraham and we can receive these blessings if we will follow His laws of prosperity.

If someone says that God doesn't want us to prosper, how can they possibly explain this verse of scripture? ". . . thou shalt remember the Lord thy God: for it is he that giveth thee power to get wealth, that he may establish his covenant which he gave unto thy fathers, as it is this day" (Deuteronomy 8:18). If it's wrong to be prosperous, *why* does God give us the power to become wealthy as part of His covenant???

16

Many people are destroyed by their wealth because they don't obtain it through following God's laws. There is absolutely nothing wrong with being prosperous and successful if we obtain and retain our prosperity as a result of following God's laws. ". . . Blessed is the man that feareth the Lord, that delighteth greatly in his commandments. His seed shall be mighty upon earth: the generation of the upright shall be blessed. Wealth and riches shall be in his house . . ." (Psalm 112:1-3). If prosperity is wrong, God certainly *wouldn't* have said that wealth and riches will be in our homes if we "fear" Him (hold Him in respect and awe) and if we follow His laws.

If someone believes that it is wrong to be prosperous, how can he explain why many of the greatest men of God were prosperous? We have already seen that Abraham was very wealthy. One of Jesus' disciples was a rich man. "When it was evening, there came a rich man from Arimathea, named Joseph, who also was a disciple of Jesus" (Matthew 27:57 *The Amplified Bible*).

Abraham and Joseph of Arimathea were wealthy. Solomon was obviously a wealthy man. There is absolutely nothing wrong with financial prosperity unless this prosperity comes ahead of God. Our Father wants us to have money, but He doesn't want money to have us!

God gave us His precious promises so we can be like He is if we follow them. "Whereby are given us exceeding great and precious promises: that by these ye might be partakers of the divine nature . . ." (II Peter 1:4). Prosperity and abundance are part of God's divine nature. He owns the whole world and everything that is in the world. He has given us more than three thousand promises in His Word so that, by these promises, we can partake of His divine nature.

God is a prosperous God and the very first chapter of the Bible says, "And God said, Let us make man in our image, after our likeness . . ." (Genesis 1:26). If God is prosperous and if He created us to be just like He is, isn't it obvious that He wants us to prosper, too?

The more we study God's Word, the more evidence we see of God's plans for our abundance and prosperity. God created great abundance when He created the earth. "Then God said, 'Let the waters teem with fish and other life, and let the skies be filled with birds of every kind.' So God created great sea creatures, and every sort of fish and every kind of bird. And God looked at them with pleasure, and blessed them all. 'Multiply and stock the oceans,' he told them, and to the birds he said, 'Let your numbers increase. Fill the earth!'" (Genesis 1:20-22 *The Living Bible*).

We can see further signs of the abundance that our Father planned for us by looking inside a watermelon, an apple, an orange, a grapefruit and many other kinds of fruit. Our Father has provided us with these seeds so that we will be able to reproduce what we use many times over. "And he said, 'Let the earth burst forth with every sort of grass and seedbearing plant, and fruit trees with seeds inside the fruit, so that these seeds will produce the kinds of plants and fruits they came from'. . ." (Genesis 1:11 *The Living Bible*).

The first chapter of Genesis tells us how God stocked the earth with fish, animals and birds and how He provided plants and fruit trees. When God

18

finished doing this, He then created a man who was meant to enjoy this abundance and to be master over the earth and everything on the earth. "Then God said, 'Let us make a man—someone like ourselves, to be master of all life upon the earth and in the skies and in the seas.'" (Genesis 1:26 *The Living Bible*).

That man was our forefather, Adam. God provided Adam with great abundance—he had everything he could ever want. However, Adam gave his riches and his dominion over all the earth to Satan. Satan was able to steal it from him because of Adam's lust and pride.

Adam forfeited the abundance and prosperity that God intends for us—His children. Satan took it away from him. This brings us to the reason why God sent His Son, Jesus Christ, to earth. Again and again I have asked Bible study classes for the precise reason that Jesus Christ was sent to this earth. Only a very small percentage knew the correct answer. Do you?

Jesus was sent here for one purpose—to *destroy* Satan's work. ". . . For this purpose the Son of God was manifested, that he might *destroy* the works of the devil." (I John 3:8). Jesus succeeded in His mission. This is why, just before ascending into heaven, He said, ". . . All power is given unto me in heaven and in earth." (Matthew 28:18).

Jesus won back every bit of power and authority that Satan had taken from Adam. He restored our abundance. Jesus paid the full price so that all His brothers and sisters can prosper. "For ye know the grace of our Lord Jesus Christ, that, though he was rich, yet for your sakes he became poor that ye through his poverty might be rich" (II Corinthians 8:9).

Some Christians believe that this verse of scripture does not refer to financial riches. They say that God is talking about "spiritual riches" here and that this does not apply to financial prosperity. I don't agree. Anyone who reads chapters 8 and 9 of II Corinthians can see that both of these chapters deal primarily with the subject of finances. Because *The Living Bible* is easy to understand, let's refer to several verses of scripture in it that come just before and just after II Corinthians 8:9.

Verse 1 speaks about the "deep poverty" and "trouble and hard times" being experienced by the churches of Macedonia. Verses 3 and 4 tell us that these churches gave much more money to Paul and his followers than they could afford to give. Verses 10 and 11 speak of finishing a project by "giving whatever you can out of whatever you have." Verses 12 and 14 speak again about the importance of giving. Chapter 9 instructs us in detail about giving to the poor and the abundance that God will give us in return.

There isn't any doubt that chapters 8 and 9 of II Corinthians deal primarily with the subject of our finances. When verse 8 tells us Jesus became poor so that we could be rich, I agree that this applies to spiritual riches. I believe the reference to financial riches is also very clear.

Some Christians use II Corinthians 8:9 to show that Jesus Christ was poor during His earthly ministry. They say that His life was a model for our lives and, because He was poor, we were not meant to prosper. I believe that is incorrect. As we examine the Scriptures carefully, I believe that many readers of this book will be surprised to see that Jesus was *not* poor when He walked on this earth two thousand years ago.

Chapter Two

Jesus Christ—Prince or Pauper?

We have discussed a verse of scripture that says, "...though he was rich, yet for your sakes he became poor, that ye through his poverty might be rich." (II Corinthians 8:9). Doesn't this tell us clearly that Jesus was financially poor during His earthly ministry? No, it doesn't say that He was poor throughout His earthly ministry. It says that He "became" poor. I believe that Jesus "became" poor when He made the supreme sacrifice on the cross at Calvary.

Jesus gave up everything at that time—even His clothing. In spite of many pictures to the contrary, Jesus was completely naked when He died on the cross. He couldn't have been any more poor than He was at that time. When He died, He didn't own one thing in this world. While He hung on the cross, Roman soldiers gambled for the clothing that He had worn.

Yes, Jesus became poor, but let's study the four gospels which tell us about His life to see how "poor" He really was. It seems apparent that Jesus was relatively poor while He was growing up as the son of a carpenter. Perhaps He was poor while He Himself was working as a carpenter. However, we are concerned here with His earthly ministry—the approximate three year period between the time He was baptized and filled with God's Holy Spirit in the Jordan River until the time He was crucified on the cross. Was He really poor during this great three year period which has changed the earth forever??? Let's examine the facts.

Some people believe that Jesus was poor because He said, ". . . Foxes have holes, and birds of the air have nests; but the Son of man hath not where to lay his head" (Luke 9:58). Jesus didn't have a home where He slept every night because He was the first traveling evangelist. He was constantly on the move.

Surely He could have stayed in the home of the wealthy Joseph of Arimathea (Matthew 27:57) or in other nice homes where He was welcomed. In fact, we'll see shortly that Jesus could have produced the money to stay each night in an inn if He had really wanted to. I believe that He slept in the open air by choice and not by necessity.

Isn't it a fact that Jesus had twelve disciples and seventy other men traveling with Him? Weren't the needs of all of these people and their families met? How can anyone say that Jesus was poor if He was able to meet the needs of such a large group of people? How many poor people run an organization of this size? How many poor people have a treasurer to keep track of their finances? Jesus and His organization had a treasurer. ". . . Judas was their treasurer . . ." (John 13:29 *The Living Bible*).

Would a poor man be able to feed large groups of four to five thousand people and their families? Jesus was a complete master of God's laws of prosperity. He used those laws repeatedly to meet

His needs. "What about the 5,000 men I fed with five loaves of bread? How many basketfuls of scraps did you pick up afterwards? 'Twelve,' they said. 'And when I fed the 4,000 with seven loaves, how much was left?' 'Seven basketfuls,' they said, 'And yet you think I'm worried that we have no bread?'" (Mark 8:19-21 *The Living Bible*). What poor man could provide for others like this?

When the tax collectors of Capernaum came to Peter and asked for money, was Jesus able to pay them? He certainly was. Here is what He said to Peter. ". . . go down to the shore and throw in a line, and open the mouth of the first fish you catch. You will find a coin to cover the taxes for both of us; take it and pay them" (Matthew 17:27 *The Living Bible*).

Jesus obviously was able to master God's laws of prosperity in order to pay His taxes and Peter's taxes. He could have used these *same* laws to produce money for *any* of His other needs, if He so chose. When Peter and the other disciples had fished all night and came up empty, Jesus was able to produce so many fish that the nets broke (Luke 5:1-11). (A similar instance is reported in John 21:1-11).

When Jesus needed a donkey to ride into Jerusalem on that first Palm Sunday, He didn't have to rent or buy a donkey. He simply told two of His disciples to go into the village of Bethpage to look for a donkey and its colt tied alongside the road. He told them to take these animals and, if anyone asked what they were doing, to say that the Lord needed them. This is exactly what happened (Matthew 21:1-7).

When Jesus needed a room to serve the Passover

meal, He didn't go to a hotel to rent one. Instead, He sent two of His disciples into Jerusalem and told them to contact a certain man who would lead them to another man. They should tell this man that they needed a large upper room and he would take care of everything. That is exactly what happened (Mark 14:12-16). How can anyone claim that Jesus was poor when He was able to obtain transportation and hotel rooms so easily?

When Jesus hung on the cross, the soldiers who crucified Him gambled for possession of His expensive, seamless one piece robe. If He was poor during His earthly ministry, where did He get a robe that was so valuable that soldiers gambled for it?

You might wonder what the connection is between the miracles performed by Jesus and His financial prosperity. The answer is that Jesus Christ had the purest faith that has ever been seen on this earth. As a result, He was able to turn little into plenty. He had absolutely no need for worldly, material assets because He knew that He could apply His faith to God's laws of prosperity in order to obtain whatever He needed.

Perhaps you are thinking, "Yes, but He is the Son of God. What does this have to do with me? I can't use God's laws of prosperity to provide miracles like Jesus did." Can't you? Jesus clearly told us that He wasn't able to perform any of His miracles with His own ability:

". . . verily, verily, I say unto you, the Son can do nothing himself" (John 5:19).

"I can of mine own self do nothing . . ." (John 5:30).

". . . the Father that dwelleth in me, he doeth the works" (John 14:10).

On many occasions, Jesus humbly told us that He couldn't do any great miracles by Himself. He was able to perform these miracles only because He yielded completely to God's Holy Spirit who lived inside of Him. You and I can also do great works here on earth—financially and otherwise—because God's Word clearly tells us that we have this same Holy Spirit living inside of us. ". . . the Spirit of Him who raised up Jesus from the dead dwells in you . . ." (Romans 8:11 *The Amplified Bible*).

Because we have the Holy Spirit in us, Jesus clearly told us, "Verily, verily I say unto you, He that believeth on me, the works that I do shall he do also; and greater works than these shall he do; because I go unto my Father. And whatsoever ye shall ask in my name, that will I do, that the Father may be glorified in the Son. If ye shall ask anything in my name, I will do it" (John 14:12-14).

Jesus Christ followed God's laws of prosperity (and all of God's other laws). He didn't rely in the least on His own ability. He relied totally upon God's Word and upon God's Holy Spirit living within Him. Because Jesus followed all of God's laws of prosperity, He enjoyed total prosperity—not just financial prosperity—but total prosperity of the spirit, soul and body—throughout His earthly ministry. John 14:12-14 tells us that we can enjoy this same total prosperity during our lives here on earth.

There is no question about it. Our Father wants His children to prosper instead of the evil sinners who now enjoy much of the world's prosperity— "The evil man may accumulate money like dust, with closets jammed full of clothing—yes, he may order them made by his tailor, but the innocent shall wear that clothing, and shall divide his silver among them" (Job 27:16-17 *The Living Bible*).

Yes, our Father wants us to prosper financially. However, this prosperity isn't "automatic" just because we're Christians. We have to follow His laws of prosperity which are carefully laid out in this book. If we follow these laws, God won't withhold any good thing from us. ". . . no good thing will he withhold from them who walk along his paths" (Psalm 84:11 *The Living Bible*). Each day He loads us down with benefits. "Blessed be the Lord, who daily loadeth us with benefits . . ." (Psalm 68:19).

Chapter Three

God's Prescription for Prosperity

I started this book with the two extreme positions that Christians have taken on the subject of financial prosperity. We have spent most of our time together so far discussing why our Father does want us to prosper financially. The time is now here to look at the other extreme—the "hyper-faith" Christians who say, "Of course God wants me to prosper! I'm going to follow His laws of prosperity and get myself a Mercedes, a $250,000 home, etc., etc."

This is not God's way. This is the way that carnal, worldly people approach the subject of prosperity. They put their selfish desires first. There isn't anything wrong with owning a nice car and nice home, but possessions must never in any way come ahead of God.

I have spent hundreds and hundreds of hours studying what the Bible has to say about financial prosperity. If I had to boil everything that I have learned down to just four words, this four word prescription for God's prosperity would be—*"Always keep God first."* Jesus told us this when He said, ". . . seek ye first the kingdom of God, and his righteousness; and all these things shall be added unto you." (Matthew 6:33). Whatever any of us need in any area of our lives, God's laws say that He will provide them to the exact degree that we keep Him first in every area of our lives.

Exactly what does this mean to always keep God first? One example of this is to never start any day without first of all spending a period of quiet time of prayer and devotion. Another example is to set definite goals of Bible study and meditation and to consistently reach these goals because this is put ahead of family time, watching television and enjoying hobbies. I ask each reader of this book to take the following short "quiz." Your honest answers will indicate whether you really are putting God first in your life:

Questions	Rate Yourself 0 to 10
1. "Do I actually place God *ahead* of each member of my family?"	————
2. "Is God *always* more important to me than my friends?"	————
3. "Do I spend *more* time seeking God each day than I do watching television or enjoying hobbies?"	————
4. "Is God more important to me than *any* possession that I have?"	————
5. "Is seeking God on a daily basis *more* important to me than seeking financial prosperity?"	————

Many Christians believe that they always keep God first, but if you will be completely honest on each of the preceding questions you might find that this isn't the case. Many Christians give God some

29

time on Sunday morning, perhaps at one or two Christian meetings each week and for a few minutes of prayer each day. In the lives of many Christians, that is "it" as far as God is concerned. Such a life style obviously does not put God first.

Many of us have accepted Jesus as Saviour, but we have never truly allowed Jesus to be Lord over every area of our lives. In order to put Jesus first, we need to deny ourselves each day and put Him first in every area of our lives. ". . . if any man will come after me, let him deny himself, and take up his cross *daily*, and follow me" (Luke 9:23).

The world's system of prosperity puts other things ahead of God—money, success, possessions and ego recognition. Every bit of this is in violation of God's laws of prosperity. Our Father wants us to prosper financially, but *only* if this financial prosperity and the things that it will buy never in any way come ahead of Him.

In order to illustrate this point, let's look at the goals of a typical, ambitious, worldly young man as he graduates from college and steps out into the world to reach his goals. What are his goals? Would you agree that many ambitious young people are seeking fame and fortune and a long life? God's Word tells us exactly how to achieve these goals— "True humility and respect for the Lord lead a man to riches, honor and long life" (Proverbs 22:4 *The Living Bible*).

Once again, we see that there isn't anything wrong with "riches" provided that they are obtained God's way. What is God's way for obtaining riches, honor and a long life? His Word says that we obtain these things by constantly *humbling* ourselves before our awesome respect for Him.

Our Father does want us to enjoy riches, honor and long life as long as we reach these goals as a result of keeping Him first by always humbling ourselves before Him. This is God's "prescription" for prosperity in every area of our lives.

Our Father wants us to surrender our lives totally to Him. ". . . put Him in complete charge of everything there is . . ." (Hebrews 2:8 *The Living Bible*). He doesn't want us to put family, money, hobbies or anything else ahead of Him. "Thou shalt have no other gods before me" (Exodus 20:3).

The world's system of prosperity puts money and the things it can buy ahead of God. In fact, many people get so caught up with earning money that they think about it almost constantly—money is the center of their lives. Their lives revolve around money. It consumes them. It drives them constantly. If they're not thinking about making money, they're thinking about how to invest it or what they can buy with it. Although most of these people don't realize it, money has become their god. It takes first place in their lives. They can't get enough of it. The more they get—the more they want.

This all-consuming desire for money is exactly the kind of desire that we should have for God. We should think about Him all the time. He should be at the very center of our existence. Every aspect of our lives should revolve around Him. We shouldn't ever be able to get enough of Him—the more we learn of God and His ways, the more we should want to learn.

This is the way to prosperity. ". . . as long as he sought the Lord, God made him to prosper" (II Chronicles 26:5). We'll never want for anything as long as we constantly put the Lord first and keep Him first. ". . . they that seek the Lord shall not want any good thing" (Psalm 34:10).

The world searches eagerly for wealth and for recognition from other people, but these things come from God. When we are in right standing with Him and we love Him ahead of everything else and always keep Him first, we'll receive all of the riches and honor that we'll ever want or need. "I love them that love me; and those that seek me early shall find me. Riches and honour are with me; yea, durable riches and righteousness" (Proverbs 8:17-18).

Many of us have fallen into the trap of not keeping God first. In fact, many of us allow the problems in our lives to take predominance over God. Too many of us think, "I need this," "I've got to have that," and "I don't know how to solve this problem."

Instead, we should say "God, I'm going to put you first and *keep* you first every hour of every day of my life. I'm going to study and meditate constantly in your Word and do exactly what it tells me to do, trusting completely in you to supply every one of my needs."

Too many Christians (often without even realizing it) are much more problem-centered than they are God-centered. We spend too much time focusing on our problems and too little time focusing on Almighty God and His ability to solve every one of our problems to the exact degree that we can let go of these problems and give them to Him and trust Him to solve them.

If God *really* is first in our lives, *why* should we *ever* be worried about any problem? If we are worried about any problem, isn't it a fact that we are actually allowing that problem to take first place ahead of God??? Instead of constantly focusing on the problems, we should focus constantly on the great promises of God's Word and the great ability of God's Holy Spirit living inside of us.

All freedom comes from switching our preoccupation from ourselves to God. God's Word clearly tells us to keep our minds focused on Him and to trust completely in Him—"Thou wilt keep him in perfect peace, whose mind is stayed on thee: because he trusteth in thee." (Isaiah 26:3).

A peace is available to us that is "perfect"—a a total, complete and absolute peace! Perfect peace certainly includes freedom from financial problems. How can any of us have that peace if we worry about financial problems?

God's two requirements for perfect peace are very clear. First, we must keep Him first at all times. We must keep our minds focused on Him at all times—and *not* on our problems. Second, we must trust Him completely. We must pay the price to find out what His Word says He will do and then believe that He *will* do what He says He will do.

God's laws of prosperity will only work to the degree that we keep Him first in our lives—totally, completely and absolutely ahead of everything else. They are based on total dedication of our lives to Him. The blessings that we receive from our Father will be in direct proportion to the degree of our true, deep and lasting commitment to Him.

Chapter Four

God's Way or the World's Way?

God's laws of prosperity are founded upon the basic fact that He owns everything and that we own *nothing*. Do you think that you own your car? . . . your home? . . . and the other possessions which, according to man's laws, you own? God's ways are usually quite different from man's ways and this is a specific example. God's Word clearly tells us that we don't "own" anything.

It is very important to grasp the concept that we don't "own" anything and that God just lets us "use" things. Then God's laws of prosperity will start to fall into place. We came into this world empty-handed and we will leave this world the same way. "For we brought nothing into this world, and it is certain we can carry nothing out" (I Timothy 6:7).

While we are here, God allows us to make use of possessions which actually belong to Him. ". . . the heaven and the heaven of heavens is the Lord's thy God, and the earth also, with all that therein is" (Deuteronomy 10:14). Every bit of money on this earth is owned by God, not by us. "The silver is mine, and the gold is mine, saith the Lord of hosts" (Haggai 2:8).

God owns everything in heaven, everything on earth and everything in between. He owns the sun, the moon, the stars and all the planets of the universe. Our money belongs to God. All the things that we think we own belong to God. We ourselves belong to God. "The earth is the Lord's, and the fulness thereof; the world, and they that dwell therein" (Psalm 24:1).

Some people will read these statements and think, "My possessions belong to me. I earned them. I worked hard to get them. I can do what I want with them." God's Word says, "And thou shalt say in thine heart, My power and the might of mine hand hath gotten me this wealth. But thou shalt remember the Lord thy God: for it is he that giveth thee power to get wealth . . ." (Deuteronomy 8:18).

Most people who have become wealthy following the *world's* system of prosperity don't understand this concept. This is why God's Word says that it is so difficult for most wealthy people to enter into God's kingdom. ". . . how hard it is for them that trust in riches to enter into the kingdom of God! It is easier for a camel to go through the eye of a needle, than for a rich man to enter into the kingdom of God" (Mark 10:24-25).

The key words here are the words "trust in riches." This is the world's way. God's laws of prosperity require us to trust in Him instead of trusting in riches. The world's way is to trust in material assets and to continually try to accumulate more of them. The more of these assets we have accumulated, the harder it is for us to enter into God's kingdom.

It's interesting to note exactly what the words *eye of a needle* mean. Many of the ancient cities of the Middle East were surrounded by high walls. These walls had large gates. When darkness came, these gates were closed and locked so that enemies could not attack the cities. However, a provision was made for late arriving travelers to enter through a small door in the gate.

That door was called a "needle's eye." It could be opened so one man at a time could get in, but it was impossible for a large number of soldiers to rush through. Late-arriving travelers usually arrived on camels. The only way that a camel could get through the door was by being completely unloaded of all of its goods and getting down on its knees. Then a camel could just barely squeeze through the "needle's eye."

This is what Jesus was referring to in Mark 10:24. A rich man can enter into God's kingdom, but it isn't easy. Like a camel, the rich man has to be completely "unloaded" of all his worldly possessions (acknowledge God's ownership) and get down on his knees before God (surrender to Jesus and put Him first). Only then can the rich man enter into God's Kingdom.

The world's system of prosperity is a full 180 degrees from this. In the world, millions of people think everything would be just great if they could only have unlimited funds. However, close observation of people who have more money than they can spend shows they they don't find any lasting satisfaction from their wealth. It is foolish to think that the world's prosperity satisfies. The more we get the more we want. "He that loveth silver shall *not* be satisfied with silver, *nor* he that loveth abundance with increase: this is also vanity" (Ecclesiastes 5:10).

Worldly possessions never satisfy. God didn't make us that way. True satisfaction can only be found deep within ourselves, not in any external worldly possessions. Benjamin Franklin was a great thinker. He once said, "Money has never made a man happy yet, nor will it. There is nothing in its nature to produce happiness. The more a man has, the more he wants. Instead of filling a vacuum, it makes one. If it satisfies one want, it doubles and triples that want in other ways."

The world's prosperity is empty. Most people who become rich without following God's laws of prosperity sooner or later think, "I've got everything that I ever wanted and then some. How come I'm not happy and fulfilled? I feel so empty inside. Is this all there is to being wealthy??"

We see many people who have prospered by the world's system of prosperity who have family problems—divorce, spoiled children, adultery, etc. Others experience severe problems as they approach death and ponder over their worldly estates—riches which soon must be given up to be fought over by selfish heirs and heiresses. Other wealthy people find that the years of pursuing wealth have given them high blood pressure, ulcers, heart disease or other illness. Everyone who prospers by methods other than God's laws of prosperity sooner or later will find that this prosperity will become a curse. ". . . the prosperity of fools shall destroy them" (Proverbs 1:32).

What is a fool? God's Word gives this definition of a fool: "The fool hath said in his heart, there is no God . . ." (Psalm 53:1). Many people who are financially successful acknowledge God with their heads, but not with their hearts. Their hearts are caught up with making money and with the things it can buy. In reality money is their god. This is why

37

man's methods of prosperity eventually destroy the people who follow them. Prosperity apart from God brings trouble. "In the house of the righteous is much treasure, but in the revenues of the wicked is trouble" (Proverbs 15:6).

The world's system of prosperity has its price. It doesn't turn out the way men think it will. Financial prosperity achieved by the world's methods will bring sorrow, but God's Word clearly teaches us that God's laws will enable us to prosper in every area of our lives *without* any sorrow. "The blessing of the Lord, it maketh rich, and he addeth *no* sorrow with it" (Proverbs 10:22).

Where does sorrow come from? We have just seen that it doesn't come from following God's laws of prosperity. As we saw previously, God's Word tells us that sorrow comes from loving money—from putting money ahead of Him. "For the love of money is the root of all evil: which while some coveted after, they have erred from the faith, and pierced themselves through with many sorrows" (I Timothy 6:10).

When we covet money and the things that it will buy, we "err from the faith"—we go away from God, from always putting Him first and trusting completely in Him. God's Word tells us that people who do this will be "pierced" with many sorrows.

The love of money isn't limited to the rich. Many people who don't have much money still love it. They still want it more than anything else in their lives and would do almost anything to obtain large amounts of it. These people are often tempted by "get rich quick" schemes. God's Word says that "get rich quick" schemes are evil. "He that hasteth to be rich hath an evil eye . . " (Proverbs 28:22).

God's Word warns us over and over against "coveting"—against being greedy, always wanting more. God hates covetousness. ". . . the covetous, whom the Lord abhorreth" (Psalm 10:3). God wants us to hate covetousness, too. His Word says that this kind of thinking will cause us to prolong our days. ". . . he that hateth covetousness shall prolong his days" (Proverbs 28:16).

Our Father doesn't want our lives to center around money and the things that money will buy. His Word tells us that the accumulation of money and possessions is wrong and that this will hurt us. "There is a sore evil which I have seen under the sun, namely riches kept for the owners thereof to their hurt" (Ecclesiastes 5:13).

Millions of Christians have never really had to trust God for their finances—especially Christians in the middle and upper income classes. Too many of us have lived a lifetime based upon worldly job security backed up by such things as bank accounts, investments, equity in property, pension and profit-sharing plans, insurance, etc.

I'm not saying that these things are wrong, but I am saying that they have tended to insulate millions of people against learning and applying God's laws of prosperity. We've got to stop placing our trust in our various financial "cushions" and start trusting in God. God wants very much to supply all of our needs during the difficult times which many economists believe are coming. He'll always do His part, but we must do our part.

God's laws of prosperity will show us exactly how to "profit" during the coming economic crisis. ". . . I am the Lord thy God which teacheth thee to profit, which leadeth thee by the way that thou shouldest go" (Isaiah 48:17). No matter how bad our economy might get, God's laws of prosperity, if followed exactly will provide us with financial substance that we need.

If and when difficult economic times do come upon us, we will not solve our problems by "storing up" money and possessions. If we store up riches, we violate one of God's most important laws. The more we amass, the more we show our trust in what we have stored up instead of trusting in God.

One example of this is the hoarding that always becomes prevalent in difficult times. During wars and other crises, many people hoard whatever is in short supply. We saw this with sugar, gasoline, silk stockings and other items in World War II. We saw another example of this in the gasoline shortages of 1973.

Hoarding is always caused by fear—trusting in whatever we're stockpiling instead of trusting in God. We're starting to see a lot of hoarding today as people anticipate the hard times that are ahead. Some people are storing up large amounts of dehydrated food and canned goods. Others are storing up large amounts of gold, silver and precious gems in anticipation of a possible collapse of the world monetary system.

It really concerns me to see many spiritual leaders advocating this. Some churches are selling "tribulation food." Some Christian leaders are advising us to convert everything that we can to precious metals and gems. Is this spiritual?? This is the *world's* way of doing things! Hoarding is caused by fear and preoccupation with ourselves which is opposed to the instructions in God's Word which teach us to put God first, other people second and ourselves last.

God's ways are diametrically opposed to the world's ways. Instead of trusting in worldly riches, our Father clearly wants us to trust in Him and to share what we have with others. "Charge them that are rich in this world, that they be not highminded, nor trust in uncertain riches, but in the living God, who giveth us richly all things to enjoy; that they do good, that they be rich in good works, ready to distribute, willing to communicate" (I Timothy 6:17-18).

So far we have discussed primarily "why" God wants us to prosper and "why" God's ways differ from the world's ways. Now the time has come to switch our emphasis from "why" God wants us to prosper to "how" God wants us to prosper. There is one step which must be taken before we make the transition from "why" to "how." That is to "renew" our minds—to learn how to change our long-established thought processes from the world's methods of prosperity to God's laws of prosperity. Let's see what God's Word has to say about this important subject.

Chapter Five

God Wants Us to Renew Our Minds

One of the biggest obstacles to learning and applying God's laws of prosperity is the tremendous difference between them and the world's system of prosperity. Many of us have followed the world's system for many years and it's not easy to change from long-standing habit patterns.

However, that is exactly what we must do. In order to understand and apply God's laws of prosperity, we must stop conforming to the world's system and "renew" our minds with God's laws of prosperity. If we do this, we'll be handling our finances exactly the way our Father wants us to and our lives will be transformed. ". . . be *not* conformed to this world: but be ye *transformed* by the *renewing* of your mind, that ye may *prove* what is that good, and acceptable, and perfect will of God" (Romans 12:2).

What does the word "renew" mean? It means *to make new*. It means to completely change. For example, when we see urban renewal in one of our cities, that portion of the city is totally altered. It is made "brand new." This is what we must do with our minds before we can understand and apply God's laws of prosperity.

Our minds are like computers and they must be "reprogrammed" with God's laws of prosperity. Most of us need to feed a great deal of new data into these "computers." Are you willing to "erase" the tapes which have governed your lifetime financial habits so that you will line up with God's laws of prosperity instead of the world's system of finances?

If you are, God says that this will "transform" your life. This means that your life will be "completely changed." In fact, the Greek word *metamorphoo* (which means a *metamorphis*—a complete change) that is used in Romans 12:2 is the very same word that is used in Matthew 17:2 and Mark 9:2 to describe the "transfiguration"—the complete change—of Jesus Christ. This gives us some indication as to how greatly our lives can be transformed by the proper renewal of our minds.

Our Father, like any worldly father, wants very much for His children to prosper and to be successful and healthy. In fact, His Word says that he wants this "above all things"—more than anything else. "Beloved, I wish above all things that thou mayest prosper and be in health, even as thy soul prospereth" (III John 2).

Of course our Father wants us to be successful, healthy and prosperous, but did you notice the five word "qualifier" at the end—"even as thy soul prospereth?" Many people who quote this particular verse of scripture seem to *stop* with the word "health." We must *not* leave out the final five words. These last five words are the *cause* of the prosperity and health that our Father wants so much for us.

We will experience this prosperity and health that He wants so much for us in exact proportion to the degree that our souls are "prospered"—to the exact degree that our souls are made brand new. What is the "soul?" The soul is the combination of our minds, our wills and our emotions. In order to prosper, our souls must prosper and in order for our souls to prosper they must be made "brand new"—they must be reprogrammed with information from God's Word.

A prosperous soul is a soul that is filled with God's Word. God wants us to constantly engage in the process of converting our souls from the world's ways to His ways. If we follow God's laws, even the most simple child will receive our Father's wisdom. "The law of the Lord is perfect, *converting the soul:* the testimony of the Lord is sure, making wise the simple" (Psalm 19:7).

God's laws will never change. *We* are the ones who have to change. In order to prosper, we have to change from the way that we have always handled our finances to the way that our Father tells us to handle our finances. The time to do this changing is now. Prosperity will be "automatic" for us when we get to heaven.

All of God's children will enjoy His prosperity and abundance in heaven. However, prosperity obviously isn't "automatic" here on earth. If it was, we wouldn't ever see Christians with financial problems. If we want to prosper here on earth, our minds *must* be renewed. Our souls *must* be brought into line with God's laws of prosperity.

What exactly must be done so that our souls will prosper? This question is clearly answered in verses 2 through 4 of III John. Instead of stopping

44

with verse 2 as many people do, let's look at all three of these verses together. "Beloved, I wish above all things that thou mayest prosper and be in health, even as thy soul prospereth. For I rejoiced greatly, when the brethren came and testified of the truth that is in thee, even as thou walkest in the truth. I have no greater joy than to hear that my children walk in truth."

The key word is the word "truth." God's Word tells us exactly where to find "truth. ". . . thy word is truth" (John 17:17). The only place to find truth is in the Word of God. Verse 3 tells us that our Father wants His truth inside of us (deep down in our hearts) and that He wants us to walk in truth (live our daily lives based upon the teachings of His Word). Verse 4 tells that nothing gives Him greater joy than to see His children walking in truth.

This is so clear! We will prosper under God's laws of prosperity to the exact degree that we fill our hearts with these laws and obey them in our daily lives. This isn't as easy as it might seem. Most of us will have to change considerably from the way that we have handled our finances in the past. We often nullify the effectiveness of God's laws because of our "tradition"—because of the way that we have always done things. "Making the word of God of none effect through your tradition . . ." (Mark 7:13).

As we constantly line up our thoughts, feelings, and emotions with God's Word, we will think and talk and act more and more like our Father thinks and talks and acts. Our Father doesn't ever think about financial or other shortages. There is no place for such thinking in His mind and He doesn't want us to allow any of that kind of thinking into our minds.

45

If our minds are continually filled with thoughts of doubt and unbelief, how can we possibly enjoy prosperity in our lives? God wants us to renew our minds because He wants to restore our souls—to make them "brand new." "The Lord is my shepherd; I shall not want. He maketh me to lie down in green pastures: he leadeth me beside the still waters. He *restoreth my soul . . ."* (Psalm 23:1-3).

When the Lord is our shepherd—when we are the sheep and He is leading us—completely in charge of every aspect of our lives, we will *not* want for anything. He will guide us to the still waters— away from the angry waves of the failing systems of the world. He will restore our souls so that we will always be aligned with His laws of prosperity instead of frantically worrying about the constant erosion of the world's man-made system of prosperity.

Our souls must be restored. Our souls must be made new. We must get rid of our old ways and start out anew. "Strip yourselves of your former nature—put off and discard your old *unrenewed* self—which characterized your *previous* manner of life and becomes corrupt through lusts and desires that spring from delusion; And *be constantly renewed* in the spirit of your mind—having a *fresh* mental and spiritual attitude . . ." (Ephesians 4:22-23 *The Amplified Bible).*

We must clean up our minds. We must renew them. We must make them fresh and new. Too many of us are trying to solve serious problems with our limited, carnal, unrenewed minds. Our minds may be fine for the normal, everyday situations that we face, but when a serious problem comes along, our unrenewed minds are insufficient.

46

Our Father doesn't want us trying to figure everything out with our limited, unrenewed minds. His Word tells us that we shouldn't rely upon our own understanding. Instead, He wants us to know what His Word says to do and then to do what His Word tells us to do, trusting completely in Him. "Trust in the Lord with all thine heart; and *lean not unto thine own understanding*. In all thy ways acknowledge him, and he shall direct thy paths" (Proverbs 3:5-6).

Christians who haven't renewed their minds in God's Word don't have the "spiritual eyesight" to see their way out of seemingly unsolvable problems. In order to solve the really difficult problems of life, we have to put on our "spiritual eye glasses." We have to see these problems as God sees them.

There are *no* problems—financial or otherwise—that are impossible for God. ". . . with men this is impossible: but with God *all* things are possible" (Matthew 19:26). There are *no* problems that we can't solve through Jesus Christ. "I can do *all* things through Christ which strengtheneth me" (Philippians 4:13).

Our Father doesn't want us surrendering to the problems that overwhelm so many people. Jesus Christ paid the price at Calvary to give us victory over all problems. ". . . in the world ye shall have tribulation: but be of good cheer; I have *overcome* the world" (John 16:33). "Many are the afflictions of the righteous: but the Lord delivereth him out of them *all*" (Psalm 34:19).

Our Father gave us His Word which is full of instructions which tell us exactly what we need to do in order to overcome the problems of this world. He gave us His Holy Spirit to live inside of us and to guide us in the understanding of the truth that is contained in His Word. ". . . when he, the Spirit of truth, is come, he will guide you into all truth . . ." (John 16:13).

Christians who have paid the price of diligently renewing their minds will focus in on the solution. Non-Christians and Christians who haven't paid the price of renewing their minds focus in on the problem. "The thoughts of the diligent tend only to plenteousness; but everyone that is hasty only to want" (Proverbs 21:5).

Renewal is a law of God. We renew our bodies each day with breakfast, lunch and dinner. We renew ourselves each night through sleep. God wants us to do the same things in our spiritual lives. All of us are growing older physically and God's Word clearly tells us that we should offset this aging process by renewing ourselves spiritually each and every day of our lives. ". . . though our outward man perish, yet the inward man is *renewed day by day"* (II Corinthians 4:16).

In the physical world, when we eat our meals, this food is transformed into physical strength and energy. The same principles apply in the spiritual realm. We need to feed our spirits each and every day with spiritual food from God's Word. If we do this, that spiritual food is transformed into a spiritual strength and energy which is called faith.

We should "feast" on God's Word. We should "stuff" ourselves with it. Jesus told us that we should feed ourselves with *every* word from our Father so that we can live our lives as He wants us to live them. ". . . Man shall not live by bread alone, but by *every* word that proceedeth out of the mouth of God" (Matthew 4:4).

48

If we do this spiritual feeding on a regular and continuing basis, regardless of what we might be going through on the outside, we will always be full of joy on the inside. "Thy words were found, and I did eat them; and thy word was unto me the joy and rejoicing of mine heart" (Jeremiah 15:16).

Our Father doesn't want our imaginations running rampant about the financial problems of the world and how bad they might become. He wants our minds renewed to the point where they can cast down these negative thoughts and focus totally on the promises in His Word. *"Casting down* imaginations, and every high thing that exalteth itself against the knowledge of God, and bringing into captivity *every* thought to the obedience of Christ"... (II Corinthians 10:5).

If we don't continually renew our minds, we leave them wide open to doubts, fears and anxieties about the worldly situations that surround us. Our souls cannot prosper unless our minds are under control and our minds won't be under control unless we can cast out all negative imaginations and bring every one of our thoughts completely in line with the Word of God. If our minds are properly renewed, *we* will decide what we are going to think about. We will *refuse* to let any external situation control our thought process.

Too many Christians focus so much on the problems of the world that they ultimately become part of those problems because they are so identified with them. Instead of focusing so much on the problems that surround us, we need to redirect our attention to the solution. "Finally, brethren, whatsoever things are true, whatsoever things are honest, whatsoever things are just, whatsoever

49

things are pure, whatsoever things are lovely, whatsoever things are of good report; if there be any virtue and if there be any praise, *think on these things"* (Philippians 4:8).

Our Father has more than enough to meet every one of our needs. Too many of God's children are focusing on inflation, interest rates and unemployment instead of meditating constantly upon His promises. God's Word *isn't* dependent in any way upon the condition of a man-made economic system!

We can live peaceful, joyous, prosperous, healthy lives in this world. Jesus Christ has paid the price for our peace, our joy, our prosperity, and our health. However, once again, this peace, joy, prosperity and health are not "automatic" while we are on this earth. We will experience them only to the degree that we renew our minds on a daily, continuing basis.

In order for us to prosper as our Father wants us to prosper, our souls must prosper. In order for our souls to prosper, God's Word must dominate our lives. God's instructions to us must be the absolute center of our lives. Everything that we think and say and do must revolve around His instructions to us.

Chapter Six

How Do We
Renew Our Minds?

Now that we have seen that our Father wants us to renew our minds, we need to see exactly how He tells us to do this. We renew our minds through constant study and meditation in God's Word. Everyone wants to prosper, but *few* people are willing to pay the necessary price of study and meditation in God's Word which is necessary in order for His laws of prosperity to be manifested.

If I could speak personally to each reader of this book I would ask you, "Do you want God to approve of what you do?" You undoubtedly would say, "Yes, of course I do." Here is how we win our Father's approval. "Study to shew thyself approved unto God, a workman that needeth not to be ashamed, rightly dividing the word of truth" (II Timothy 2:15).

We win God's approval by studying His Word! We win His approval by working hard enough at this study so that we won't be ashamed. I ask you—do you believe that God has approved of your Bible study during the past week??? . . . during the past month??? . . . during the past year??? Are you ashamed at the amount of time that you spend studying the instructions that our Father has given to us?

There isn't any "easy way." Bible study is hard work. None of us should expect our Father to prosper us unless we are willing to pay the price of working hard at studying His Word. In fact, the Greek word *spoudazo* which is translated *study* in II Timothy 2:15 means *exertion, diligence*. In Hebrews 4:11 this same Greek word is translated to mean *labour*. There is no question that our Father expects us to work hard studying His Word.

Everything that any of us will ever need to know is contained in God's Word. If we have problems in one particular area of our lives, we need to do a thorough job of "rightly dividing" God's Word in order to find every possible verse of scripture that covers this particular area. For example, in this book, I have "rightly divided" the Bible on the subject of financial prosperity. Studying the Bible isn't a high-flying, supernatural experience. There are a few times like this, but Bible study is often laborious and tedious. This is especially true for someone who isn't accustomed to studying the Bible.

It's difficult to get started studying the Bible. It usually takes quite awhile to learn how to enjoy Bible study. Unfortunately, I have found that the great majority of Christians quit before they get to that point. The Bible will make us think like we have never thought before . . . but only if we're willing to dig and dig and dig without expecting it to unfold its secrets immediately.

What is the difference between "studying" the Bible and just "reading" the Bible? My business partner, Ed Hiers, once gave me an interesting comparison between reading the Bible and studying the Bible. Ed said that if he had a book titled

How To Survive When You're Lost In The Woods he might just "read" it if he was reading it in the comfort of his home. However, if he really was lost in the middle of a large forest and his life depended upon survival, he'd do much more than just "read" this book. He'd "study" it very thoroughly. He'd "devour" every fact in this book that could possibly show him how to get out of this predicament.

This is precisely what God wants us to do with His Word. Because of the difficult economic times that many economists are predicting, all of us should study what God's Word has to say about prosperity. We need to devour it. We need to learn everything that we possibly can about how to avoid or solve the financial problems that soon will come upon this world. Millions of Christians are living far beneath their rights and privileges and children of God because they fail to pay the price of constantly studying God's Word in order to find out exactly what these rights and privileges are and how to attain them in their lives.

Specifically and exactly, how do we go about studying the Bible? This is a subject that would make a book by itself. I have covered this subject in detail on my two forty-minute cassette tapes titled *How To Study The Bible*. Write to the publisher of this book for information on these and other cassette tapes on the Bible.

Briefly, let me summarize the contents of these tapes in a few paragraphs. I want to start by saying that I don't believe that there is any one method of studying God's Word. I know several mature Christians who use different methods of studying the Bible. The methods may vary considerably, but I have always found that the *princi-*

ples of effective Bible study are similar regardless of the method that is used.

I personally use the "subject" method of studying the Bible. I decide the subjects that I need to learn more about. For example, here are a few subjects in alphabetical order: Anger, Faith, Fear, Forgiveness, Joy, Love, Patience, Prayer, Prosperity, Worry. Whatever our individual needs might be, I believe that each of us needs to "rightly divide" God's Word to find everything that we can on this particular subject.

In my cassette tape, I explain in detail how to use the various versions of the Bible, a reference Bible, a Bible concordance, a topical Bible, a Bible dictionary, Greek and Hebrew lexicons and other Bible study tools. All of these tools are available to help us "dig out" every possible verse of scripture on any given subject and then to understand exactly what these verses of scripture mean.

In this book, I have "dug out" dozens and dozens of verses of scripture on the subject of financial prosperity. I have explained what these verses of scripture mean. This part has already been done for you. Next, let's discuss what it means to "meditate" on these verses of scripture. Let's start by looking at two verses of scripture that tie the words *meditate* and *prosper* together. The first one says, "This book of the law shall not depart out of thy mouth; but thou shalt meditate therein day and night, that thou mayest observe to do according to all that is written therein: for then thou shalt make thy way prosperous and then thou shalt have good success" (Joshua 1:8).

This is one of the most important verses of scripture in the entire Bible for anyone who is interested in prosperity and success. In fact, it is the *only* verse of scripture in the entire Bible which contains the words *prosperous* and *success.*

I have worked with many Christians in the area of prosperity and success and this verse of scripture has been one of the most significant verses in showing them the three things that our Father tells us to do if we intend to be prosperous and successful:

(1) We must speak His Word constantly—His scriptures should constantly come out of our mouths.

(2) We should constantly study His Word and meditate "day and night" on what it says.

(3) We should live our lives exactly as His Word tells us to live them. We should know His Word so well that we conduct our lives "according to all that is written therein."

The second place that we find scripture that ties meditation and prosperity together is at the very start of the Book of Psalms. "Blessed is the man that walketh not in the counsel of the ungodly, nor standeth in the way of sinners, nor sitteth in the seat of the scornful. But his delight is in the law of the Lord; and in his law doth he meditate day and night. And he shall be like a tree planted by the rivers of water, that bringeth forth his fruit in his season; his leaf also shall not wither; and whatsoever he doeth shall prosper" (Psalm 1:1-3).

First, God tells us that, if we want to prosper in everything we do, He will bless "the man that walketh not in the counsel of the ungodly." God will bless us if we will follow His laws of prosperity instead of following the world's methods of prosperity.

God doesn't want us living the way the sinful

world lives. He doesn't want us looking at things the way worldly people do. We have already seen in Romans 12:2 that He tells us not to conform to the world's way of doing things, but, instead, to transform our lives by following His laws.

How do we do this? We do this by loving His Word so much that we actually "delight" in it. Because of this great "delight" we just can't get enough of God's Word. We'll be so hungry and thirsty spiritually that we'll meditate day and night in His Word in order to find out everything that we possibly can about our Father's laws for living our lives.

What will happen to us if we do this? God's Word tells us that we will be like a tree planted next to a river. No matter how bad a drought might be, the leaves of such a tree will never wither and dry up because the roots of this tree will be able to draw water from the river. So, no matter how bad a drought may be, the trees that are next to a river will always continue to bear fruit.

Many economists believe that a "financial drought" is coming over our land. Inflation, recession, unemployment and all the rest are already causing our economy to start to "wither." However, in the midst of such a drought, Christians can still thrive. We can still bear fruit. We can still prosper in everything that we do if we have meditated day and night in God's Word so that our "roots" reach deep into our Father's laws of prosperity.

Unfortunately, many Christians will "wither" financially during this financial drought. Many Christians will be destroyed because of lack of knowledge of God's laws. "My people are destroyed for lack of knowledge . . ." (Hosea 4:6). If Christians want to be delivered from this financial "drought" they can be delivered in exact proportion to their knowledge of God's laws of prosperity. ". . . through knowledge shall the just be delivered" (Proverbs 11:9).

Now that we have seen how Joshua 1:8 and Psalm 1:1-3 tie "prosperity" and "meditation" together, let's look at this word "meditation" in more detail. Exactly what does meditation mean and exactly how do we go about meditating in God's Word? Once again, I don't believe that there is any "one way" of doing this. However, I'd like to share with you a system of meditation that has worked wonderfully for me and for many other Christians who have followed it.

This system starts with reading and studying the Bible in order to find every possible verse of scripture on one subject—in this case, the subject of financial prosperity. Once all of these verses of scripture are found, I believe that the process of meditation on these verses should start by typing or neatly printing each of these verses on a 3" x 5" file card.

I recommend this size card because it will fit easily into a man's shirt pocket or a woman's purse. You can easily carry these cards with you throughout the day. Once these cards are completed, then I suggest that you arrange your stack of file cards in the order of their importance to you—the ones that mean the most to you on top, the next most important verses in the middle of the stack, etc.

Next—and this is important—take just *one* of these cards at a time. Don't fall into the trap of "spiritual indigestion" by trying to digest too much of God's Word at one time. Take only one verse of scripture with you and meditate on that one verse of scripture throughout that day and night. Don't rush. God is never in a hurry. He wants us to be calm and quiet in our meditation in His Word.

I believe that meditation means to fix our attention on a particular verse of scripture and to turn this verse of scripture over and over in our minds—looking at it from every angle. I believe that meditation means to "personalize" a verse of scripture—to think deeply about how each particular verse of scripture applies to our own lives.

When we meditate on a verse of scripture, our thought process should be something like this: "What does this verse of scripture mean?" "What is God telling me?" "Exactly how does this apply to my life?" "What changes do I need to make in my life in order to do what God is telling me to do?" "What am I going to do differently today? . . . this week? . . . this month? . . . during the next year?"

This is so beautiful. Unlike the meditation that people do in transcendental meditation, yoga and similar forms of meditation which tell us to "empty" our minds, we are, instead, meditating by "filling" our minds with the awesome power of the Word of God. As we meditate more and more on God's Word, this meditation brings us more and more in touch with our Creator.

This process of daily meditation isn't easy at first. When we're not used to something, it takes time for it to become part of our daily habit pattern. Be patient with this system of meditation. Give it a fair chance to become part of your daily habit pattern.

Most readers of this book have jobs that require you to work approximately eight hours each day.

This means that most of us can't "study" God's Word throughout the day. However, we certainly can "meditate" on it constantly. We can meditate on it while we're getting dressed in the morning, while we're driving to work, during our lunch hour, while we're driving home, etc.

Some people work at occupations which will enable them to meditate on God's Word while they are working. In addition, all of us have discretionary time at the end of each day's work and on weekends that can be used to meditate on God's Word.

During these times of meditation, in addition to personalizing these verses of scripture by turning them over in our minds, we also should *speak* these verses of scripture over and over with our mouths. In fact, the Hebrew word that is translated *meditate* in Joshua 1:8 and Psalm 1:2 actually means *to murmur* or *to mutter.*

When God's Word tells us to "meditate day and night," this means that we should constantly open our mouths and *speak* the verse of scripture that we are meditating on. We should do this over and over and over—day and night. As we constantly speak a verse of scripture, this helps us to memorize this verse of scripture. Also, as we constantly speak a verse of scripture, this releases the power of that verse of scripture.

Be sure to meditate on just one verse of scripture at a time. Turn it over and over in your mind. Think how it applies to your particular need. Say it out loud—over and over and over. Memorize it. Keep doing this until it becomes a part of you— until you know it so well that it has gone from your

Bible to your 3" x 5" card to your mind and then down into your heart.

This should always take at least one full day. Sometimes, this will take several days. Don't rush this process. Even if you finish only one verse of scripture a week, you still will have *fifty* great teachings from God deep down in your heart at the end of one year.

This system has worked beautifully in my life. I have worked with several people who have followed it and the results have been exceptional in their lives, too. Many times when I happen to meet Christians who are following this system, they smile and pull out the 3" x 5" file card that they are carrying that particular day.

If your mind hasn't been renewed, this might sound like a lot of drudgery. However, God's Word tells us that this continuous meditation eventually will be just the opposite of drudgery. Psalm 1:2 told us that we should meditate day and night in God's Word because we "delight" in His laws. What will happen to us if we "delight" in God's Word and "meditate day and night" in it? Here is the answer: "Blessed is the man that feareth the Lord, that delighteth greatly in his commandments. His seed shall be mighty upon the earth: the generation of the upright shall be blessed. Wealth and riches shall be in his house; and his righteousness endureth for ever" (Psalm 112:1-3).

God's Word should be an absolute delight to us because His Word tells us everything that any of us will ever need to know in order to live good lives here on this earth. ". . . as you know Him better, He will give you, through His great power, everything you need for living a truly good life: He even shares His own glory and His own goodness with us!" (II Peter 1:3 *The Living Bible*).

Once we fully understand what this means to us, we won't be able to get enough of God's Word. We'll be *so* delighted that we'll *gladly* meditate day and night in His Word. If we do this continually, we will prosper in *every* area of our lives—financially, spiritually, physically, mentally and emotionally.

Chapter Seven

God's Perspective
On Work and Discipline

God's Word repeatedly tells us that He expects us to work and discipline ourselves if we want to lead prosperous, successful lives. For some reason, many Christians believe that they can have anything that they ask for in Jesus' Name and they they don't have to work hard.

This is incorrect. God's Word clearly tells us that we need to do the very best that we can with the abilities that God has given us and *then* we should stand solidly on our faith in God to take care of the rest. ". . . having done all, to stand" (Ephesians 6:13).

God's laws of prosperity definitely require us to work hard if we want to prosper. This may sound obvious, but it is a fact that the work ethic upon which this country was founded has eroded more and more with the passage of time. On the whole, there is much more of a "the world owes me a living" attitude today than there was just one generation ago.

In today's society, many people are content to put as little into their work as they think they can get away with. This is one of the primary reasons why our economy has the problems that it has. Too many employees are receiving a full day's pay for less than a full day's work. This cost is passed on to the consumer and this is one of the primary causes of inflation.

In our society, more and more emphasis is being placed on fun, enjoyment and leisure—on a "me first—what do I want to do to please myself today?" attitude. Many people have been able to get by with this type of attitude for many years, but the pendulum is now starting to swing the other way. I believe there will be much more necessity to work hard in the years immediately ahead of us than there has been in most of our lifetimes.

God's Word says, ". . . if any would not work, neither should he eat" (II Thessalonians 3:10). This obvious truth has been contradicted by the top-heavy, unbalanced systems that have been developed in many of our welfare programs, governmental agencies and some labor unions. Many of these governmental systems and labor union goals were predicated upon basic Christian principles. However, over a period of time, many self-seeking leaders, consumed by greed and corruption, have made them a mockery of what their founders intended.

The price is now about to be paid. In the United States, we live in a society that has virtually done away with the lower class. This is not scriptural. Jesus said, ". . . ye have the poor always with you..." (Matthew 26:11). Many people at the bottom of the economic ladder in the United States have color television sets, more than adequate living quarters and much more than the basic necessities of life. That would be fine if they had earned what they have. However, many of these people don't work and they wouldn't if they were given an opportunity to work.

If we want to succeed, we need to eliminate the "short cuts" which eventually cause poverty. If we want to succeed, we must work hard and diligently. "He becometh poor that dealeth with a slack hand: but the hand of the diligent maketh rich" (Proverbs 10:4). "Seest thou a man diligent in his business? He shall stand before kings . . ." (Proverbs 22:29).

God's Word tells us that we should work hard and that we should show the world around us the virtues of hard work. ". . . work with your hands, as we charged you; so that you may bear yourselves becomingly, be correct and honorable and command the respect of the outside world, being (self-supporting), dependent on nobody and having need of nothing" (I Thessalonians 4:11-12 *The Amplified Bible).*

Today, many people have little or no initiative. They're not self-starters and they always need to have someone tell them what to do. God's Word tells us that we should work like an ant works. He tells us that the ant has no boss, but it instinctively works hard to provide its needs. God then compares this to lazy humans who take it easy and doze a lot. He warns us that this attitude will lead to poverty:

"Go to the ant, thou sluggard; consider her ways, and be wise: which having no guide, overseer, or ruler, provideth her meat in the summer, and gathereth her food in the harvest. How long wilt thou sleep, O sluggard? When wilt thou arise out of thy sleep? Yet a little sleep, a little slumber, a little folding of the hands to sleep: so shall thy poverty come as one that travelleth, and thy want as an armed man" (Proverbs 6:6-11).

The day of reckoning is drawing near. Proverbs 6:9-11 tells us that one day lazy people will wake up and find that poverty has overtaken them and, just like an armed robber, this poverty will take everything they have from them—the financed homes, cars and everything else that they thought they "owned."

We cannot continue to violate God's laws. No matter how "square" they might seem to the society in which we live, these laws are from God. We may get away with breaking His laws for awhile, but sooner or later we're going to pay the price. Employers can't continue to pay people more than they are worth. Sooner or later the bubble has to burst. This philosophy has already resulted in widespread unemployment in several industries which have driven wages of both skilled and unskilled workers to a much higher level than is justified.

If we are constantly trying to get paid more than our work is worth, we are violating God's laws of prosperity. In fact, God clearly instructs us to go in the opposite direction. Instead of robbing our employers by doing less than we're capable of doing, God's Word tells us to work as hard as we possibly can, "Whatsoever thy hand findeth to do, do it with thy might . . ." (Ecclesiastes 9:10).

Instead of doing less than we have to do, our Lord wants us to go "all out." He wants us to do more than we have to do. If we need to go one mile, Jesus told us that we should go two miles. "And whosoever shall compel thee to go a mile, go with him twain" (Matthew 5:41). Jesus told us that we should do twice as much as we are required to do.

This is just the opposite of the prevailing attitude in our world today.

Many people are looking for ideal working conditions, longer vacations, more leisure, etc. God's Word tells us to get out and do our job if it's cold (or wet or uncomfortable or for any other reason). If we don't do this, we will not receive any lasting gain. "The sluggard will not plow by reason of the cold; therefore shall he beg in harvest, and have nothing" (Proverbs 20:4).

Whatever type of work any of us might do, God's Word tells us that we should put everything we have into it because we really are working for Jesus Christ, not whomever our worldly employer might happen to be. "And whatsoever ye do, do it heartily, as to the Lord, and not unto men . . ." (Colossians 3:23).

It's interesting that God's Word tells us to do our work "heartily." This means that we should do our work from our hearts . . . from our spirits . . . our innermost beings. That's where the Holy Spirit lives. If we allow him to take charge of our work, we'll do a great job no matter what line of work we are in.

The Holy Spirit is the world's best salesman, the world's best mechanic, the world's best factory worker, the world's best engineer, the world's best nurse, the world's best doctor, the world's best dentist, etc., etc. There is no limit to what He can do through us in any occupation. Our job is to do the very best we can with the human abilities that He has given us and then to trust in Him for the rest.

If a Christian doesn't do his best at his work, he soon starts to get an empty feeling. This comes from God's Holy Spirit inside of us "nudging" us to get to work. On the other hand, when we put in a good solid day's work, we get a sense of inner satisfaction. This is because, way down deep, we know that we're doing what our Father wants us to do.

God wants us to do our best, but the fact is that the great things of life really are done through us, not by us. "Except the Lord build the house, they labour in vain that build it . . ." (Psalm 127:1). God will do great things through us if we will first of all do our very best and then trust completely in Him to take it from there. Many Christians miss out by going to one extreme or the other. Either we don't do our best or we think that we have to do everything by ourselves and we don't "let go and let God."

Hard work starts with discipline. If we want to be free from financial problems or any other problems, we must have the discipline to continually study God's Word. ". . . if ye *continue* in my word, then are ye my disciples indeed; and ye shall know the truth, and the truth shall make you free" (John 8:31-32).

I ask each of you, "Do you want to be a disciple of Jesus Christ?" Do you want to be free? We have just seen that this freedom is obtained by *continuing* in God's Word—by getting in there and staying in there—day after day, week after week and month after month. In my opinion, the one primary thing that stops Christians from realizing the freedom that is ours in Christ is lack of consistency. Many Christians start studying God's Word, but there aren't many Christians who continually study and meditate in God's Word.

The words *disciple* and *discipline* come from the same root. This isn't a coincidence. If we really want to be disciples of Jesus Christ, we must have the discipline to get into God's Word and stay there. We will only do what God's Word tells us to do if we get into His "perfect law of liberty"—the law that sets us free—and continually study and meditate in these laws. If we do this we will be blessed by our Father. ". . . whoso looketh into the perfect law of liberty, and *continueth* therein, he being not a forgetful hearer, but a doer of the word, this man shall be *blessed* in his deed" (James 1:25).

If it takes us four years to graduate from worldly high schools and another four years to graduate from college, *why* should any of us expect to learn God's great spiritual laws without spending a great deal of time and effort studying and meditating in God's Word??? If we want God to prosper us, we must give ourselves *wholly* to continual study and meditation in His Word. "Meditate upon these things; give thyself *wholly* to them; that thy profiting may appear to all" (I Timothy 4:15).

Many Christians decide that they are going to pay the price of continuous spiritual study and meditation, but they just don't stick to it. The first four or five weeks are the hardest. If we can stick to a definite pattern of study and meditation for at least that long, we will start to develop habit patterns that will continue.

Some Christians believe that this disciplined study and meditation is contrary to a life that is led by God's Holy Spirit. They say, "I'm not going to grind it out every day. I'm just going to wait on the Holy Spirit each day and do what He leads me to do."

This is fine, but God's Holy Spirit never leads us contrary to the teachings of God's Word and God's Word tells us again and again about the absolute importance of disciplining ourselves to study and meditate constantly in His Word. Satan wants us to have sloppy day-to-day habits with no set pattern. Our Father wants us to realize how precious our time is. "Teach us to number our days and recognize how few they are; help us to spend them as we should" (Psalm 90:12 *The Living Bible*).

Our Father doesn't want us to waste the time that He has given us. He wants us to make good use of it. "Look carefully then how you walk! Live purposefully and worthily and accurately, not as the unwise and witless, but as wise, sensible intelligent people; making the very most of the time—buying up each opportunity—because the days are evil" (Ephesians 5:15-16 *The Amplified Bible*).

Now that we have studied what God's Word says about the importance of hard work and discipline, let's see what God's Word says about the results that diligent study and meditation will produce in our hearts, in our mouths and and in our actions.

Chapter Eight

Prosperity in
Our Hearts and Mouths

When we hear God's Word spoken, this sows a seed in our hearts. Unfortunately, many people hear God's inspired Word and, as they leave the meeting where they heard this, they have forgotten most of what they heard before they reach their parked automobiles. When this happens, the seed of God's Word never has the opportunity to take root and grow. God's Word will only grow in our hearts to the degree that we constantly meditate on it.

"Head knowledge" isn't sufficient to activate any of God's laws. God's laws come from a spiritual realm that is completely different from the natural world that we live in. We can't understand God's laws with our minds. Our Father doesn't want us trying to figure out His laws with our human understanding. The key to activating His laws is to get them down inside of our heart. ". . . as he thinketh in his *heart*, so is he" (Proverbs 23:7).

This is why God wants us to meditate day and night in His Word. When we work diligently at meditating in God's Word this will change every aspect of our lives because the significant events in our lives are based upon what we believe deep down in our heart. "Keep thy heart with all diligence; for out of it are the issues of life" (Proverbs 4:23).

Our Father wants us to fill our hearts and our minds with His Word. ". . . lay up these my words in your heart and in your soul" (Deuteronomy 11:18). Constant meditation on God's Word causes the scripture to drop from our minds down into our hearts. As this process takes place, the problems that used to baffle us won't be able to trip us up any more. "The law of his God is in his heart; *none* of his steps shall slide" (Psalm 37:31).

As I have mentioned, in difficult economic times, many people try to stockpile money and hoard up food and other necessities of life. This urge to "store up" is actually a worldly manifestation of the spiritual "storing up" that our Father wants us to do. He wants us to fill our hearts to overflowing with His Word so that we will react instinctively to it whenever we are faced with a crisis.

Our Father wants His Word to be so solidly established in our hearts that we won't be afraid of any problems that come upon us. ". . . the righteous shall be in *everlasting remembrance.* He shall *not* be afraid of evil tidings: his heart is *fixed*, trusting in the Lord. His heart is *established*, he shall *not* be afraid . . ." (Psalm 112:6-8).

We should never be afraid of "evil tidings." Instead of focusing on bad news about inflation, unemployment, interest rates, etc., our hearts should be "fixed" upon God's Word, trusting completely in His promises. Our hearts should be solidly "established" in God's Word. No matter how bad the situation might look, a truly established heart will never waver.

Our Father wants our minds and our hearts to be so full of His Word that it will overcome any problems that come into our lives. "So mightily grew the Word of God and prevailed" (Acts 19:20). The Greek word that is translated *prevail* means to be strong and powerful. Our Father wants His Word to be so strong and powerful inside of us that it will prevail over every problem that comes against us.

There is nothing to fear. There is no need to worry. No matter how bad a situation might seem to be, God will always come through to the exact degree that we believe in Him deep down in our hearts. God will do His part if we do our part. Our part is to get enough of His Word in our hearts so that we will be able to trust totally and completely in Him. "The Lord is good, a stronghold in the day of trouble; and he knoweth them that trust in him" (Nahum 1:7).

Our minds are like computers and our hearts are where the data for these computers is stored. When a problem comes into our lives, our minds should immediately turn to the storage area in our hearts and search out the appropriate law of God that will affect the problem that we are faced with. Then, we should react based upon our faith in what God's Word says and not upon the problem that we are confronted with.

No matter how difficult the problem might seem to be, we should trust the Lord. God's Word tells us that He doesn't want us to be "careful." This old English word that was used in the King James Bible doesn't mean the same as the word *careful* does today. This word means to be *full of care*—to be worried or anxious.

When difficult problems come into our lives, instead of being full of worries and cares, our Father wants us to go to Him with a prayer of faith that is based solidly upon the promises in His Word. If we really trust Him, then we will thank Him as we pray because we know that He will do what His Word says He will do.

If we will follow these instructions when troubles come into our lives, God's Word says that *we will receive a peace that is so great that it will be beyond our human understanding.* "Be careful for nothing: but in every thing by prayer and supplication with thanksgiving let your requests be made known unto God. And *the peace of God, which passeth all understanding,* shall keep your hearts and minds through Christ Jesus" (Philippians 4:6-7).

If we really do trust God deep down in our hearts, we'll show this trust by the words that come out of our mouths. We have just seen a good example of this regarding our prayers in times of adversity. God's Word has a lot more to say about the importance of the words that come out of our mouths.

If our hearts are filled to overflowing with God's Word, this abundance of scripture has to come out of our mouths. Jesus told us this when he said, ". . . out of the abundance of the heart the mouth speaketh. A good man out of the good treasure of the heart bringeth forth good things: and an evil man out of the evil treasure bringeth forth evil things" (Matthew 12:34-35).

In times of extreme pressure, we will show what fills our hearts by the words that come out of our mouths. God's Word tells us what happens when we allow the wrong words to come out of our mouths.

"If any man among you seem to be religious, and bridleth not his tongue, but deceiveth his own heart, this man's religion is vain" (James 1:26).

The Greek word that is translated *vain* means to be void of results. Thus, if we don't "bridle" our tongues (keep them under control), this can cause our Christianity to be ineffective—to be void of results. If we constantly allow words to come out of our mouths that are contrary to God's laws, this will stop our heavenly Father from prospering us.

Many Christians put themselves into "financial jail" and "throw away the key" because of the words of fear and doubt that come out of their mouths when they are faced with a crisis. They don't realize that God's Word says, "Thou art snared with the words of thy mouth, thou art taken with the words of thy mouth" (Proverbs 6:2). A "snare" is a trap and many of us are trapped by our words without even realizing it. Our words can put us into financial prison or they can set us free. "Whoso keepeth his mouth and his tongue keepeth his soul from troubles" (Proverbs 21:23).

In moments of stress, we can't control our tongues with sheer will power. ". . . the tongue can no man tame . . ." James 3:8). When the going is tough, we can't control what we say by our minds. Our words are totally controlled by what we believe in our hearts. This is why it is so important for our hearts to be filled with God's Word.

Do you remember our discussion of Joshua 1:8, the only verse of scripture in the entire Bible that mentions the words "success" and "prosperous" in the same verse? This verse of scripture begins with the words "This book of the law shall not depart out of thy mouth . . .". This means that, if we expect to

74

prosper, we should speak God's Word all day long every day of our lives—it shouldn't ever "depart" from our mouths.

I ask each reader of this book to be honest with yourself and to ask yourself two questions: "Do I really speak the Word of God all day long from the time I get up in the morning until the time that I go to bed at night?" "Do I do this day after day, week after week and month after month?"

God's Word is greater than any problem that any of us will ever face. In the spiritual realm, God's Word, backed by strong, patient, unwavering faith, has the same power as if God spoke these words Himself and this will cause us to prosper. "So shall my word be that goes forth out of my mouth: it shall not return unto me void, but it shall accomplish that which I please, and *it shall prosper* in the thing whereto I sent it" (Isaiah 55:11).

We can clearly see that God's Word ties together the words that we speak with our mouths and the prosperity that we receive in our lives. God will prosper us if we deeply believe His promises in our hearts and if we constantly open our mouths and speak these promises. We should *never* talk about tight money, hard times or other financial problems. If we allow these words to come out of our mouths, we are actually denying the promises of God. How can we expect our Father to bless us if we constantly open our mouths and deny the promises that He has given to us???

I urge each reader of this book to apply this concept to the procedure we covered previously. Take a verse of scripture on a 3" x 5" filing card with you each day. Meditate on this verse of scripture throughout the day and night. Turn it over and over in your mind. Think exactly how this applies to your life. Above all else, open your mouth and boldly speak this verse of scripture—over . . . and over . . . and over.

When the going is tough, that's exactly when we need to speak God's Word more . . . and more . . . and more. When I was a brand new Christian on the very edge of bankruptcy and a nervous break-down, I used to say my favorite verse of scripture (Philippians 4:13) over and over and over. I can remember dark and dreary days when I would sit down at my desk and say "I can do all things through Christ which strengtheneth me" one hundred times. Every time that I'd say this I'd write down the number on a pad . . . 1 . . . 2. . . . 3 . . . 4, etc. and I kept going until I reached #100. This wasn't easy. Try it sometime and see for yourself.

God's Word tells us how our faith grows. ". . . faith cometh by hearing, and hearing by the word of God" (Romans 10:17). God's Word says that our faith grows by hearing God's Word. We are also told that some people hear God's Word and do not profit. "For unto us is the gospel preached, as well as unto them: but the word preached did not profit them, not being mixed with faith in them that heard it" (Hebrews 4:2).

Many people can go to a meeting where the gospel is preached and this preaching of God's Word will profit some of the people, but not all of the people. Hearing God's Word will only profit us to the degree that we mix this with faith. How do we "mix this with faith?" The answer is that we must speak what we believe and we must act on what we believe. I am absolutely convinced that our faith will grow much more rapidly when our ears hear our own mouths constantly speaking God's Word.

When we face difficult problems our words must express our faith. We must not waver. We must hold fast to the confession of God's Word because we know that our Father will do exactly what His Word says He will do. ". . . let us hold fast the profession of our faith without wavering: for he is faithful that promised . . ." (Hebrews 10:23).

We're all human. We're not perfect. We might slip and allow something negative to come out of our mouths. If this happens, we should go immediately to our Father and confess the error of our ways and ask Him to forgive us. He will do this, "If we confess our sins, he is faithful and just to forgive us our sins, and to cleanse us from all unrighteousness" (I John 1:9).

If we ask our Father to forgive us He will. He will completely cleanse us from these words. He will render them null and void. It will be as if they were never spoken. He'll forget that we said them. "For I will be merciful to their unrighteousness, and their sins and their iniquities will I remember no more" (Hebrews 8:12).

Chapter Nine

Doing What Our Father Tells Us To Do

The time has now arrived to take action on the final instruction of Joshua 1:8—the "Prosperity Scripture." Joshua 1:8 tells us, (1) to meditate day and night in God's Word, (2) to speak God's Word constantly and, (3) " . . . to *do* according to *all* that is written therein . . . "

Jesus Christ placed great emphasis on the importance of doing what God's Word tells us to do. "Therefore whosoever heareth these sayings of mine, and *doeth* them, I will liken him unto a wise man, which built his house upon a rock: And the rain descended, and the floods came, and the winds blew, and beat upon that house; *and it fell not:* for it was founded upon a *rock.* And every one that heareth these sayings of mine, and *doeth them not,* shall be likened unto a foolish man, which built his house upon the *sand:* And the rain descended, and the floods came, and the winds blew, and beat upon that house; and it *fell:* and *great* was the fall of it" (Matthew 7:24-27).

Many economists predict that great economic storms will be coming upon us. Will you fall under the pressure of these storms? Jesus says that we won't fall if we do what His Word tells us to do

78

because then our foundation will be built upon solid rock.

However, it is a sad fact that many Christians hear God's Word, but fail to do what it says to do. When this happens, Jesus says that we are building on a shaky foundation of sand and we will fall. Our financial future in a shaky economy will finally come down to one great truth—are we actually doing what God's Word tells us to do?

Obedience is the key to receiving God's blessings. ". . . blessed are they that hear the word of God, and *keep* it" (Luke 11:28). Many Christians fail to receive their Father's blessings simply because they don't step out in faith and do what His Word says to do.

This is what "separates the men from the boys" spiritually. Strong faith demands action. If we really believe, then we'll do exactly what our Father's Word tells us to do. ". . . be ye *doers* of the word, and *not* hearers only, deceiving your own selves" (James 1:22).

If we just listen to God's Word and don't do what it says to do, we deceive ourselves!!! Why does God tell us to fill our hearts and our mouths with His Word? He tells us this for one reason. ". . . the word is very nigh unto thee, in thy mouth, and in thy heart, that thou mayest *do* it" (Deuteronomy 30:14).

When we surrender our lives to Jesus Christ, we are given a recreated spirit—a brand new spiritual heart. This will cause us to want to do what God's Word tells us to do. "A new heart also will I give you and a new spirit will I put within you: and I will take away the stony heart out of your flesh, and I will give you an heart of flesh. And I will put my spirit within you, and cause you to walk in my statutes, and ye shall keep my judgments, and *do them"* (Ezekiel 36:26-27).

God will recreate our human spirits. He also will put His Holy Spirit inside of us to help us to obey Him and to guide us in following His Word. ". . . it is God who is all the while effectually at work in you—energizing and creating in you the power and desire—both to will and to work for His good pleasure and satisfaction and delight" (Philippians 2:13 *The Amplified Bible).*

As we yield our lives to God's Holy Spirit within us and as we study and meditate continually in God's Word, we'll do much more than just memorize verses of scripture. We'll do exactly what God's Word tells us to do and, as a result, our Father will bless us in everything that we do. " . . . if anyone keeps looking steadily into God's law for free men, he will not only remember it but he will *do* what it says, and God will greatly bless him in everything he *does"* (James 1:25 *The Living Bible).*

One time Jesus was surrounded by great crowds of people and His disciples came to Him and told Him that His mother and His brothers were waiting to see Him but couldn't get to Him because of the tremendous crowds. Jesus replied, ". . . my mother and my brethren are these which hear the word of God and *do* it" (Luke 8:21). Is Jesus Christ your "big brother?" He has clearly told us that He expects His brothers (and sisters) here on this earth to *do* what God's Word tells us to do. There is no other way to prosper under God's laws of prosperity. If we expect to prosper, then we need to do what God's laws tell us to do. ". . . *keep* the law of the Lord thy God. Then shalt thou prosper, if thou takest heed to fulfill the statutes . . . " (I Chronicles 22:12-13).

We can enjoy prosperity and pleasure here on this troubled earth if we'll just do what our Father tells us to do and live our lives as His Word tells us to live them. "If they *obey* and serve him, they shall spend their days in prosperity, and their years in pleasures" (Job 36:11).

Again and again, God's Word ties the words "prosper" and "prosperity" to the word "do." If we do what God's Word tells us to do, we are told that we will prosper at everything that we do and in every direction that we turn. "And *keep* the charge of the Lord thy God, to walk in his ways, to keep his statutes, and his commandments, and his judgments, and his testimonies, as it is written in the law of Moses, that thou mayest *prosper* in all that thou doest, and whithersoever thou turnest thyself . . ." (I Kings 2:3).

If we will obey His instructions, our Father will enable us to "eat the good of the land"—to enjoy the best that this world has to offer. "If ye be willing and *obedient*, ye shall eat the good of the land . . . " (Isaiah 1:19).

Would you like to live a long life—a good, full, peaceful complete life? God's Word tells us exactly how to do this. "My son, forget not my law; but let thine heart *keep* my commandments: for length of days, and long life, and peace, shall they add to thee" (Proverbs 3:1-2).

God's Word tells us exactly how to live a long life that is filled with peace. It says that we need to learn the teachings of His Word and then to do what His Word tells us to do. Then we will live long lives that are filled with peace.

Let's look closely at three words in Proverbs 3:2—"length of days." When I first looked at these words I thought that they meant long life. However, that isn't true because the words "and long life" immediately follow these words. Then I realized that this means that, if we obey God's Word, He will guide us so that we will be able to get a lot more done each day.

This is exactly what has happened in my life. For the past nine years I have spent great amounts of time studying and meditating in God's Word and doing my best to live my life the way that His Word tells me to. During this time, I have seen amazing changes in my time control. I'm doing much more today than I ever did before, yet I do it with a lot more ease and much better overall balance in my life than ever before.

Even though my daily schedule is a full one, I'm able to get everything done that needs to be done and still enjoy good balance in my life in the areas of family time, recreational time, exercise, etc. It is true—the Lord will bless us with longer and fuller days to the exact degree that we are obedient to His Word.

God's Word tells us that we can actually put ourselves in a position where His blessings will "come on" us and "overtake" us. We don't have to chase after God's blessings! His Word says that they will pursue us and overtake us. "And it shall come to pass, if thou shalt hearken diligently unto the voice of the Lord thy God, to observe and to *do* all his commandments which I command thee this day, that the Lord thy God will set thee on high above all nations of the earth: and all these blessings shall come on thee and overtake thee, if thou shalt hearken unto the voice of the Lord thy God" (Deuteronomy 28:1-2).

How beautifully all of this comes together. Our Father tells us that He wants us to "hearken diligently" to His voice in order to find out how He wants us to live our lives. Then He tells us that we need to do exactly what His Word tells us to do. If we do this, He says that He will "set us on high." He will place us in a realm of spiritual knowledge that will put us above the way most people on earth live their lives. If we do what our Father's Word tells us to do, we are told that His blessings will come after us and overtake us.

It's up to us. God has given all of us freedom of choice. He has given us His laws of prosperity. They are outlined in specific detail in this book. If we follow them, we will prosper in every area of our lives. If we turn our backs on them and insist on living our lives in our own way, then we must be willing to pay the penalty for our disobedience.

Many Christians *think* that they know God's laws, but their *words* and their *actions* show that they *don't.* We will be tested constantly in this life and our test results will be based, not upon what we think we know, but on what we actually say and do during these tests of life.

One way that God will test each of us is in the handling of our money. He can clearly see how we observe His instructions by observing what each of us does in an area that is very important to all of us—our finances. The rest of this book will outline in detail the various tests that all of us must pass in regard to the way that we handle our finances.

We are told exactly what our Father wants us to do with our money. If we follow every one of these instructions, we will prosper in all areas of our lives regardless of the world's economic situation.

Chapter Ten

We Reap What We Sow

All of the remaining chapters in this book will be based upon one Biblical principle—God's laws of sowing and reaping. These laws started when God created the earth and they will never cease as long as the earth lasts. "While the earth remaineth, seed time and harvest, and cold and heat, and summer and winter, and day and night shall not cease" (Genesis 8:22).

Jesus told us that every area in the kingdom of God is based upon the principle of sowing and reaping. He said that we plant seeds in the ground and that they sprout and grow even though we can't understand how all of this works. "And he said, So is the kingdom of God, as if a man should cast seed into the ground; and should sleep, and rise night and day, and the seed should spring and grow up, he knoweth not how" (Mark 4:26-27).

We all know how God's laws of sowing and reaping work in the area of planting seeds for flowers, fruits and vegetables. Let's see how these same laws of sowing and reaping work in other areas of our lives. The basic verse of scripture on sowing and reaping simply tells us, ". . . whatsoever a man soweth, that shall he also reap" (Galatians

6:7). If we want carrots, we have to plant carrot seeds. If we want corn, we have to plant corn seeds. If we want tomatoes, we have to plant tomato seeds. This is very obvious. However, God's laws of sowing and reaping go far beyond the agricultural realm. They apply to every area of our lives.

For example, consider a husband who believes that his wife doesn't love him enough. How can he receive more love from her? Should he demand that she love him more? Should he insist on it? Should he try to force her to show more love? If we want to "reap" anything, God's Word tells us that we have to "sow" seeds. What kind of seeds should we sow if we want more love?

Jesus gave us the answer when He gave us "The Golden Rule." ". . . all things whatsoever ye would that men should do to you, do ye even so to them: for this is the law . . . " (Matthew 7:12). If we want to receive more love, we first of all must plant seeds of love ourselves. We will reap exactly what we sow.

If we want others to love us more, we need to start by loving others more. "A man that hath friends must shew himself friendly . . . " (Proverbs 18:24). This principle works in the area of love. It also works in the area of faith. When Jesus taught us about faith, He compared it to a "seed." ". . . If ye have faith as a grain of mustard seed . . . " (Matthew 17:20). If we sow enough seeds of faith and patiently wait for our "crop" to come in, we will receive a harvest from the "faith seeds" that we have planted.

None of us want to reap a poor harvest in our lives, but God's laws of sowing and reaping work both ways. The same ground that gives us a beautiful tulip will also produce ugly weeds. Many of us have sown seeds of anger, criticism or unforgiveness. A a result, other people have been angry, irritable and critical towards us. We reap what we sow.

Many of us have been sowing "crops" in many areas of our lives for many years without realizing it. It's not difficult to determine exactly what kind of crops we have been planting. Jesus told us how to find out when He said, ". . . by their fruits ye shall know them" (Matthew 7:20).

If we have planted seeds of love, faith and kindness, we can tell this by the results—the "fruit" that we are receiving in our lives. On the other hand, if we have been planting the other kind of seeds, we can also tell this by the negative results that we receive in our lives. ". . . as thou hast done, it shall be done unto thee: thy reward shall return upon thine own head" (Obadiah 1:15).

How could God's laws of sowing and reaping be any clearer? Whatever we want to receive more of, we first of all need to "sow" more of that very thing. All of us have seen how God's laws of sowing and reaping apply to seeds planted in the ground. We now can also see how these same laws apply to the areas of love, kindness, anger, criticism, etc.

However, many Christians have failed to realize that these very *same* laws of sowing and reaping apply to our *finances*. If we want to reap a harvest of money, we must sow seeds of money. God's laws of sowing and reaping work exactly the same in the financial realm as they do in the agricultural realm and in the realm of human relations.

We should never hesitate to do good things with any attributes that we possess. God's Word tells us that whatever good thing we do for others, He will give back to us. ". . . whatsoever good thing any man doeth, the *same* shall he receive of the Lord" (Ephesians 6:8).

Whenever we give our abilities, our love, our kindness or our money, what we are really giving is a portion of ourselves. When we give of ourselves, this plants a seed which gives our Father "the channel" that He needs in order to give back to us under His fair and impartial laws of sowing and reaping.

Let's look into God's Word for some facts which will clearly show us how God's laws of sowing and reaping apply to our finances. Let's start with the one verse of scripture that perfectly describes the financial prosperity that our Father has available for His children who follow His laws of prosperity. I've used the Amplified Bible version of this because I believe that it does an excellent job of amplifying the total prosperity that is available to us if we follow God's laws of prosperity.

"God is able to make all grace (every earthly blessing) come to you in abundance, so that you may always and under all circumstances and whatever the need, be self-sufficient—possessing enough to require no aid or support and furnished in abundance for every good work and charitable donation" (II Corinthians 9:8 *The Amplified Bible*).

Isn't this magnificent? We are told that our Father is able to abundantly provide every blessing in our lives so that, no matter what happens, we can always have *every* one of our needs met with enough left over for *every* charitable donation that we are led to give.

God's Word not only says that this type of

87

prosperity is available to us, but we are told that this is "always" available to us "under all circumstances." In other words, no matter what the world's economy is doing, our Father is still able to provide abundantly for us.

Let's take a look at this same verse of scripture in the King James version. I have never seen a verse of scripture with more positive statements. It is full of words such as "all," "always," "every" and "abound" (which come from the same root Greek word which is translated *abundance*). Let's look at the seven positive words in this one short verse of scripture—I have italicized each of these words in order to place emphasis on them:

"And God is able to make *all* grace *abound* toward you; that ye, *always* having *all* sufficiency in *all* things, may *abound* to *every* good work" (II Corinthians 9:8).

How can God's Word be any clearer? How much promise can be contained in one short verse of scripture? I never cease to be thrilled at all of the strong, powerful, positive words in this verse of scripture.

However, there is one key word at the start of this verse that must be discussed and that is the word "able." We are not told that God will always provide all of this for us. This isn't "automatic" for all Christians. If it were, we would never see any Christians with financial problems.

This verse of scripture says that God is "able" to provide great prosperity for us, but it doesn't say that He will. What changes God's "is able to" to "God will?" Do you know the answer?

The answer isn't hard to find. All that we need to do is to read the two verses of scripture which immediately precede the beautiful promises of verse 8. The King James version shows this very clearly. Let's look at all three verses together to see the whole picture. "But this I say, he which soweth sparingly shall reap also sparingly; and he which soweth bountifully shall reap also bountifully. Every man according as he purposeth in his heart, so let him give; not grudgingly or of necessity: for God loveth a cheerful giver. And God is able to make all grace abound toward you; that ye, always having all sufficiency in all things, may abound to every good work . . ." (II Corinthians 9:6-8).

How do we obtain "all sufficiency in all things?" We obtain this by sowing bountifully—by sowing many financial seeds as a result of giving cheerfully to the Lord. When we do this, God's Word tells us that we will reap bountifully in return and we will always have "all sufficiency in all things."

In order to reap this harvest of God's blessings, we must sow the seeds. If we sow sparingly, we will reap a modest harvest. If we sow bountifully, cheerfully and ungrudgingly, God will supply abundantly so that we will always have everything that we need with enough left over to contribute to every good work.

God wants us to sow seeds by giving money *not* for His benefit, but for *our* benefit! God doesn't need our money. He already owns the whole world and everything in it. Heaven is also His—an abundant place where people walk on streets of pure gold (Revelation 21:21).

Our Father wants us to give in order to provide Him with seeds so that He can multiply back to us. God gives us seeds to sow, not to "store up" or to hang on to. God doesn't multiply the seeds that we retain—He only multiplies the seeds that we sow.

The world's ways say that we should cling tightly on to our money so that we won't run out. God's laws of prosperity tell us that our dollars are seeds which we should plant so that He can give us a "harvest." Seeds aren't worth anything in the agricultural realm until they are planted. The same is true in the financial realm.

Jesus Christ is a perfect example of God's laws of sowing and reaping. When Jesus gave His life on the cross, He planted the greatest seed in the history of mankind. God "sowed" by giving His only Son and Jesus "sowed" by giving His life. God sowed and Jesus sowed in order to reap an ultimate harvest of hundreds of millions of people into their family—all of the people who ever have and all of the people who ever will accept Jesus Christ as their Lord and Saviour.

Jesus explained this to us when He said, ". . . I must fall and die like a kernel of wheat that falls between the furrows of the earth. Unless I die I will be alone—a single seed. But my death will produce many new wheat kernels—a plentiful harvest of new lives" (John 12:24 *The Living Bible*).

The only way that any seed can grow is for it to be buried in the ground and die. This is true in agriculture. It was true with the death of Jesus Christ. It is true in the life of every Christian. Before any of us can enter into God's family, we first of all have to "die" to the concept that we can provide our own eternal life in heaven. Instead, we have to trust Jesus for this.

This *same* principle applies to our finances. Before we can reap a financial harvest, our money must "die." We must give it up. We must sow it as we sow seeds, letting go of it and planting it. We must trust our Father to take these financial seeds and use them to produce the necessary financial harvest in our lives. We must plant the seeds for our blessings by "dying to self." This is God's law.

Some people say, "I'd like to give, but I don't have anything to give." This isn't true. God will give all of us a seed to start with and, as we sow this one seed, He will multiply it so that we will always have seeds to sow. ". . . and (God) Who provides seed for the sower and bread for eating will also provide and multiply your (resources for) sowing . . ." (II Corinthians 9:10 *The Amplified Bible*).

Each of us has to start from wherever we are financially. We need to take whatever we have to sow and sow it with faith. We need to trust God to multiply this so that He will return what we have sown and provide for our needs with enough left over to sow again.

All over the world people are trying to reap financial harvests *without* planting financial seeds. No one would ever think of going out in the summer to get some tomatoes if they hadn't planted tomato seeds in the spring. This would be ridiculous—but this is *exactly* what many people are doing with their finances!

We can't expect to withdraw from our heavenly bank account if we haven't put deposits into it. I ask each of you two questions: (1) "Do you have financial problems?" and (2) "If you do, what sort of financial seeds have you sown?" Have you sown sparingly or have you sown bountifully? ". . . He which soweth sparingly shall reap also sparingly; and he which soweth bountifully shall reap also

91

bountifully" (II Corinthians 9:6). Have you given freely or have you withheld money? "One man gives freely, yet grows all the richer; another withholds what he should give, and only suffers want" (Proverbs 11:24 *The Revised Standard Bible*).

If a farmer wants a large crop, he plants a large number of seeds. No farmer would expect a large crop if he planted only a few seeds. Why should we think that we're any different??? If we need to receive a large financial harvest, why would we plant a few (or no) seeds? This doesn't make sense.

When we have financial problems, we *can* "give" our way out of these problems! The unrenewed mind just can't understand this, but it's true. If we refuse to give freely, we are heading in the opposite direction from God. We're pulling against Him instead of pulling with Him.

If we want God to multiply back to us, we must give Him the seeds to multiply. If we need to receive a large financial harvest, we need to plant a large number of financial seeds. When I first realized this great truth nine years ago, I was in the midst of financial disaster.

Nevertheless, I started sowing financial seeds. I sowed bountifully. Day after day I'd instruct my secretary, Irene Morgan, to send contributions to various ministries. The worse our finances got, the more checks we sent. Here is Irene's account of this:

"I have been Mr. Hartman's secretary for more than eleven years. I also handle all of his finances. Nine years ago these finances were in a seemingly impossible situation. Yet, he kept telling me to send checks to his church and to various Christian organizations. The worse our finances got, the more checks we sent. It didn't make much sense to me, but I did as Mr. Hartman said. The results have been amazing. Over and over during these past nine years, whenever we have had financial problems, Mr. Hartman has increased his giving and every time—without fail—the money that we needed has come in. Sometimes we have had to be very patient, but it has always come."

We can't outgive God! However, we need to give Him a channel by which He can give to us and that channel is given to Him by the seeds that we plant through our giving. We shouldn't ever "eat" all of our seeds. No farmer would do this, and we shouldn't either. We shouldn't ever use up all of our income. We need to continuously "replant" from our income. As God gives us a harvest, we should plow it back again . . . and again . . . and again. As we give freely to God, He will give freely back to us.

If we can resist the temptation of keeping our extra seeds and, instead, continually sow them, we're on our way to prosperity following God's laws of prosperity! When the Lord starts to multiply back to us, we should take out what we need and then resist greed and selfishness. Instead of keeping the rest, we should sow abundantly from the remainder. Any Christian who will do this cheerfully and continually will find that he will always be provided for abundantly with plenty left over to continue to give to every good work (II Corinthians 9:8).

I believe that God wants His children to prosper financially for two reasons. First, I believe that our economy is going to change tremendously during the next several years. Worldly financial principles that have worked well for many years will not work well any longer and it is imperative for God's children to learn and apply His laws of financial prosperity during the difficult economic years that are ahead of us.

Second, I believe that we must learn and apply God's laws of prosperity in order to fulfil the "Great Commission" that was given to us by our Lord Jesus Christ. Jesus told us, ". . . go ye into *all* the world and preach the gospel to *every* creature" (Mark 16:15). He also said, "And this gospel of the kingdom shall be preached in *all* the world for a witness unto *all* nations; and *then* shall the end come" (Matthew 24:14).

This commission *isn't* just for missionaries. Jesus gave this commission to the entire church. Every Christian has the responsibility to see that the gospel of Jesus Christ goes out to every nation in the world.

If we aren't personally called to go into other nations to preach the gospel of Jesus Christ, then I believe that it is our responsiblity to provide financial support for those who do. It is estimated that there are more than two billion people in this world who have never heard the gospel of Jesus Christ. All Christians share the responsibility of seeing that these people are given the *same* opportunity for eternal salvation and Christian growth that we have had.

Hundreds of billions of dollars will be needed to finance this great revival of the Holy Spirit that is already beginning to spread all over the world. Hundreds of thousands of additional missionaries will be needed. World-wide revival will be paid for by millions of Christians who are willing to pay the

94

price of learning and applying God's laws of prosperity.

God's laws of sowing and reaping clearly indicate that He wants us to reap *much* more than we sow. As I have pointed out, we can see this by looking at all the seeds inside of watermelons, oranges, apples and grapefruits. Obviously, God gives us many more seeds than we need.

Our Father knows no limits. If any limits are set, we set them—not God. He wants us to stretch our faith . . . and stretch it some more . . . and more . . . and more. As we release our faith again and again, He will continually give us an increase of the money that we sow back into His kingdom. ". . . God that giveth the increase" (I Corinthians 3:7). As our Father keeps giving us an increase, we need to keep plowing it back into His kingdom. He gives us the increase. We plant this increase. He gives us more increase. We plant this increase.

On and on it goes. God doesn't want us to stop. I'm convinced that, in these last days before Jesus returns, our Father wants to raise up large numbers of Christians from all over the world who will fully grasp and utilize His laws of sowing and reaping. If we fully understand these laws and constantly apply them, the Lord will use us as a channel. Not only will He meet all of our needs regardless of what is happening in the world's economy, but large amounts of money will flow through our hands because He knows that we will constantly reinvest this money in the Kingdom of God.

Can you see this vision?? *Are you* one of the ones whom our Father wants to sow and reap over and over again, always sowing more, always reaping more and constantly planting the increase back into His kingdom? It is *awesome* to comprehend what can be done through a believing Christian who fully understands and fully applies God's laws of sowing and reaping.

Chapter Eleven

The Blessings of Tithing

God's great laws of sowing and reaping can be put into application through tithing. The word *tithe* means *one tenth* and tithing to God means giving a minimum of 10% of our income to God. In this book we will refer to tithing in terms of income, but in Bible times, tithing was done by giving the first fruits of crops, produce, cattle, etc.

God's Word tells us exactly why we should tithe. "... The purpose of tithing is to teach you always to put God first in your lives" (Deuteronomy 14:23 *The Living Bible*). As we have seen, God's laws of prosperity always keep God first while the world's system of prosperity always puts money first. Tithing is one of God's tests which clearly shows whether we *really do* keep Him first.

Here are four basic verses of scripture on the subject of tithing. "Will a man rob God? Yet ye have robbed me. But ye say, Wherein have we robbed thee? In tithes and offerings. Ye are cursed with a curse: for ye have robbed me, even this whole nation. Bring ye all the tithes into the storehouse, that there may be meat in mine house, and prove me now herewith, saith the Lord of hosts, if I will not open you the windows of heaven, and pour you out a blessing that there shall not be room enough to receive it. And I will rebuke the devourer for your sakes, and he shall not destroy the fruits of your ground; neither shall your vine cast her fruit before the time in the field, saith the Lord of hosts" (Malachi 3:8-11).

These four verses of scripture have caused a great deal of controversy among Christians. Strong proponents of tithing say that Christians who don't tithe at least 10% of their income are thieves and that Malachi 3:8-9 clearly says that we "rob" God if we don't tithe. Other Christians say that tithing is part of the Jewish law and that Christians today are no longer under this law. What is the truth? Are we required to tithe or aren't we?

It is my personal belief that it is impossible for Christians to prosper under God's system of prosperity without tithing. I don't believe that we should tithe because we feel that we "have to," but because we can clearly see that tithing is a part of God's overall principles of sowing and reaping. Abraham instituted the tithe at least four hundred years before the Jewish law went into effect.

Genesis 14:19-20 tells us that Abraham was a tither and that he was blessed by God. Abraham didn't tithe because he *had to*. He tithed because he loved the Lord and because he knew in his heart that a minimum of 10% of his "income" belonged to the Lord. I believe that we should tithe because, through Jesus Christ, we are heirs to Abraham. "And if ye be Christ's, then are ye Abraham's seed, and heirs according to the promise" (Galatians 3:29). Jesus told us that we should follow Abraham's example. ". . . Jesus said, If you were truly Abraham's children, then you would do the works

98

of Abraham—you would follow his example, do as Abraham did" (John 8:39 *The Amplified Bible*).

I believe that tithing is every bit as much of a New Testament principle as it is an Old Testament principle. In Matthew 23:23, Jesus castigated the Pharisees because they tithed and still ignored such other important things. Jesus then said that we should tithe. "Yes, woe upon you, Pharisees, and you other religious leaders—hypocrites! For you tithe down to the last mint leaf in your garden, but ignore the important things—justice and mercy and faith. *Yes, you should tithe*, but you shouldn't leave the more important things undone" (Matthew 23:23 *The Living Bible*). This verse of scripture deals with other things besides tithing, but it is interesting to see that Jesus *did* say that we *should* tithe.

How can any of us honestly say that God is first in every area of our lives and then fail to give Him at least the first 10% of "our" money??? We should give God the first part of our income and then pay our bills from the remainder. Too many people do just the opposite and then they wonder why they don't prosper. They don't prosper because they fail to follow God's laws of prosperity!

God doesn't want our "leftovers"—whatever remains after all of our bills have been paid. He wants the "first fruits"—the first 10% of our income. When we do this on a continuing basis, God will provide abundantly for us. "Honour the Lord with thy substance, and with the *first* fruits of all thine increase: So shall thy barns be filled with plenty, and thy presses shall burst out with new wine" (Proverbs 3:9-10). "Upon the *first* day of the week let every one of you lay by him in store, as

99

God hath prospered him . . ." (I Corinthians 16:2).

Our Father wants us to put Him first and then to trust Him to meet all of our needs . . . and then some. Tithing is an act of faith. It takes faith to give money off the top. It doesn't take much faith to give God whatever money is left after we have paid for everything else.

When we willingly tithe to God, this brings us into the proper relationship with him financially. We are participating in His work and we are in partnership with Him. When we tithe and meditate day and night in His Word and confess God's Word with our mouths and do what it says, we bring ourselves into partnership with God. When we do these things, we align ourselves with God's laws of prosperity and He becomes our Senior Partner. We have His wisdom and direction in every area of our finances. He is the senior partner, but He asks for a minimum of 10% of the income of the partnership and He allows us to keep 90%.

This is one of the greatest offers that God has ever made to His children! Yet, many of us try to keep 95% or 98% or 99%. Is it fair to withhold our Senior Partner's money from Him? What partnership could ever flourish if the senior partner only asked for a small percentage of the income and then the junior partner withheld part of that amount from him? Isn't this exactly what many of us are doing with our Senior Partner?

God is the greatest financial genius of all time. He always has been and He always will be. When we tithe and follow all of His other laws of prosperity, we receive His wisdom in our finances and in every area of our lives because His laws of prosperity apply to much more than just our finances.

When we tithe and follow God's other laws of prosperity, we will find that our 90% will do *more* than 100% used to do. I can tell you after several years of practical experience that 90% of our income with the blessing of God goes a lot farther than 100% without His blessing. Our Father is fully able to make 90% of our income go farther than 95% or 98% or 100% of that same income used to go. Week after week, people stand up in our Bible studies and give testimonies of the blessings that they have received as a result of their tithing. The cumulative effect of all of these weeks of testimony is absolutely awesome.

One of the most difficult things for many people to give up is their money. Our Father knows this. This is exactly why His laws of prosperity require us to release our money in order to receive financial blessings from Him. Too many Christians are looking for God to open the windows of heaven and bless them financially when they're proudly putting $5 in the collection plate each Sunday morning. God's laws of prosperity don't work this way.

We can't expect God to do the last part of Malachi 3:10 until we do the first part. There is no way that any of us should ever expect to reap a bountiful harvest without first of all sowing seeds bountifully. However, the financial offerings of most Christians cannot be called "bountiful" by any stretch of the imagination. As this is written, the latest Gallup poll shows that the average American gives a pitiful $250 a year to churches and other religious organizations! Obviously, many Ameri-

101

cans are robbing God and, as a result, they are robbing themselves!

The unrenewed, carnal mind simply can't grasp these concepts of tithing. These minds say, "If I can't pay my bills with the money that I have now, how can I possibly pay them if I give up an additional 10% of my income??" This sounds logical, but as we have seen, God's ways are much higher than man's ways (Isaiah 55:8-9). As we have seen from God's laws of sowing and reaping, when we tithe, we plant financial seeds and these seeds give God a source by which He is able to provide us with a financial harvest.

When we tithe, we honor God by putting Him first. His Word tells us that He will honor us in return. ". . . them that honour me I will honour . . ." (I Samuel 2:30). In Malachi 3:10, God challenges us to "prove" Him. This is the only place in the Bible where God gives us a challenge to "prove" Him. Why don't you "prove" God?? Why don't you tithe willingly and cheerfully for a reasonable period of time and see for yourself if God will bless you as His Word says He will??

Faith is the spiritual power that opens the windows of heaven in every area of our lives. *Why* would anyone even want to argue whether tithing is or isn't under the law when God's Word tells us that, if we tithe properly, He will ". . . open you the windows of heaven, and pour you out a blessing, that there shall not be room enough to receive it" (Malachi 3:10)??

If we really believe that God will pour out a great blessing, we certainly shouldn't try to "escape" from tithing! We should be eager to tithe! Is there *any* reader of this book who wouldn't like God to open up the windows of heaven and pour out such a great blessing that you won't have room to receive it???

The fact is that the 10% tithe is only a starting point. It isn't a maximum. Our tithe is a fixed 10%. On top of that, we can choose to give additional offerings. I believe that the tithe guarantees the harvest (meeting all of our needs) and I believe that our voluntary offerings over and above the mandatory 10% are what open the windows of heaven so that tremendous blessings are poured out upon us.

Note in Malachi 3:8 where God tells us that we have robbed Him "in tithes *and offerings*." This tells us that we can rob God not only in our mandatory 10% tithe, but also in our offerings over and above that 10%. How are we robbing Him? I believe that we are robbing Him by failing to open the windows of heaven wide enough so that He can really pour out blessings upon us!

How many readers of this book have tithed exactly 10% and still can say that God has poured out so many blessings on them that they can't even contain these blessings? I know many people who have tithed 10% who honestly can't answer "yes" to this question. God is blessing them, but they're not even coming close to receiving so many blessings that there isn't enough room to receive all of these blessings.

I *challenge you* to seek out Christians who have voluntarily increased their tithes and offerings from 10% to 15%, 20%, 25% or even more of their income and ask them if God hasn't poured out His blessings just as He said He would. ". . . He which soweth sparingly shall reap also sparingly: and he which soweth bountifully shall reap also bountifully" (II Corinthians 9:6).

I'd like to give you a factual example of this. I am a self-employed businessman and we have 25 sales representatives representing our firm. Let me tell you the story of three of these sales representatives and how they applied the preceding principles.

Most of our sales representatives are Christians, however, I believe that most of these people tithe right around 10% of their income. However, three young men (average age 33) who were not Christians when they joined our firm have since given their lives to Jesus Christ. In due time, each of these men started to tithe. Then, they started to freely give offerings on top of their tithes.

These three men currently give tithes and offerings that are far in excess of 10% of their income. Are they broke? Has this caused hardships? Not in the least—quite the contrary. All three of these men have been able to purchase beautiful homes since they became Christians and their incomes have increased by an average of almost 300% in the few short years since they started increasing their tithes and offerings.

Don't stop with 10%! Get used to tithing this amount. Prove to yourself that 90% of your income will go as far or farther than 100% used to, but don't stop there! God will pour out more blessings if you will plant more seeds.

At this point, I know that many readers are concerned about these principles because they are paid by a fixed salary. I can tell every Christian a definite way to increase income. Simply start tithing based upon what you'd like to earn rather than by what you now earn.

We have just seen that God's Word says that we *will* reap bountifully *if* we sow bountifully. *Dare* to believe this! Don't limit God because of your doubts as to whether or not your employer will increase your income. Trust God. Believe that God will do what His Word says He will do.

Don't limit God to just the income that you receive from your present employer. Our Father has many ways to increase our income if we will just release our faith and not block Him through doubt and unbelief. He might choose to increase your income through a pay raise or a bonus from your present employer. Or, he might choose to increase your income through an entirely different source.

Tithes are a fixed 10%, but offerings are governed completely by faith. Do you *honestly* believe that God will see that you will reap bountifully if you sow bountifully?? If you do, then *why* could you have any concern whatever about going well past 10%?

Once we fully comprehend these concepts, the 10% figure becomes purely academic. We can stop at 10% if we want to, but what Christian with a renewed mind would willingly stop at that level knowing that God will bless him more if he increases it? Tithing merely "primes the pump." The real blessings of God will pour out in proportion to the offerings that we cheerfully give *on top of* our 10% tithes.

Don't consume the excess. Don't "eat your seeds." Don't "store up" your seeds. Keep plowing them back until you are able to live well on 80% of your income, etc. People who steadily increase their offerings will be surprised at how easy this becomes after awhile. It was much easier for me to give 15% of my income than it was to tithe 10% and it was much easier for me to give 20% than it was to give 15%.

I have increased my tithes and offerings to the point where I now pay more income tax each year than my total yearly earnings were when I started tithing and this is just the start. My primary goal in my lifetime is to give God 90% to 95% of my income because I know that constant yearly increase in my tithes and offerings will result in an income which will meet all of my needs on only 5% to 10% of the total.

God's blessings don't stop here. They go one step further. After God tells us of the blessing that He will pour out He says, "And I will rebuke the devourer for your sakes . . ." (Malachi 3:11). The devourer is Satan. This verse of scripture tells us that, if we give freely of our tithes and offerings, God will rebuke the devourer so that "he shall not destroy the fruits of your ground." When this verse of scripture was written, God was speaking to farmers, but this same principle applies to us today whether we are farmers or whether we are in another occupation.

Whatever our line of work, God promises to rebuke Satan so that he can't destroy our fruit—the blessings that God will give us as a result of our tithes and offerings. Whatever method Satan uses to try to steal these blessings will be rebuked by God Himself. Christian businessmen who give freely of their tithes and offerings will find that they will prosper regardless of what is going on in the world's economy.

Malachi 3:11 is the only place in the Bible where God Himself says that He will rebuke the devil for us. We have the authority to do this ourselves (Luke 10:19), but when it comes to the matter of receiving blessings from our tithes and offerings, God Himself makes certain that Satan doesn't steal our blessings. Imagine how Satan must feel when God Himself stands in his way!!! How can any of us fail to give liberally if we fully understand what Malachi 3:10-11 says that God will do in return??

The principles of giving tithes and offerings apply to each of us individually and they also apply to us collectively as members of a particular church. If you know of a vibrant, growing church, check it out for yourself. I'll guarantee you that all or most of the members of that church give freely of their tithes and offerings.

Growth and tithing go hand in hand—individually and collectively. God gives every church enough people to act as a "seed." These people then have to do their part. They need to learn God's laws and apply them in their lives. If they do this properly, they will prosper and grow as individuals and their church will prosper and grow as well.

If churches would teach God's laws of prosperity and if members of their congregations would learn them and apply them in their lives, fund-raising dinners, rummage sales and similar fund-raising devices would eventually disappear. God would pour out so many financial blessings on these churches that they wouldn't be able to receive them!

These same principles apply to countries. I believe that God blesses entire countries in the same way that he blesses individuals and groups of individuals. I believe the reason that the United States has been blessed so abundantly over the years is because a far greater percentage of its people have tithed than in any other country. Also, I believe that many of the blessings of the United States have been made possible because of tax laws which provide deductions for tithes and offerings.

I believe that our churches should teach much more than they do about God's laws of prosperity. Children should be taught to give tithes and offerings from their allowances. Children should be taught to trust God to meet their needs in return.

I also believe that the local church should be the center of all of this teaching and I believe that the local church should be the recipient of our tithes. Malachi 3:10 tells us "Bring ye all the tithes into the store house . . ." The store house is the place where food is stored—the place where we are spiritually fed. If the local church is doing its job properly, this is where its members are fed spiritually each week—on Sunday mornings, in Bible study classes, in home fellowship groups and, in many churches, in Christian schools as well.

It is our obligation to give first to the local teacher. "Let him who receives instruction in the Word (of God) share all good things with his teacher—contributing to his support" (Galatians 6:6 *The Amplified Bible*). I believe that our 10% tithes should go to our local church and that our offerings on top of these tithes should go where the Lord leads us.

I believe that the local church should give freely of tithes and offerings on everything that it receives. I believe that these tithes and offerings should be given to needy individuals within the church and also to missionaries and to other ministries that the pastor, elders and deacons are led to give to. We have followed this procedure in our church and the Lord has blessed us abundantly as a result.

I am often asked if people who are seriously in

debt should pay tithes. My answer is a resounding "Yes!" Worldly logic says that the debtor can't afford to tithe. Spiritual truth says that the primary way to escape from the bondage of debt is to pay God first the money that is His and then to trust Him to give back to us to meet our needs.

I did this when I was so deeply in debt that I had to "reach up to touch bottom." This, plus meditating day and night on God's laws of prosperity, speaking them with my mouth and acting on them in my life, got me out of debt! These same spiritual principles will get anyone else out of debt if they will follow them exactly and stick with them long enough for God to turn the seeds into a harvest. God doesn't put us in financial prison. We put ourselves there! God can and will get us out if we'll follow His laws of prosperity properly.

Many people have come to me for financial counseling and I have seen these principles work many times. People who are seriously in debt are desperate. They think about their debts all the time. Their debts literally consume them. I know what they're going through. I have been there.

Step by step I take these people through God's laws of prosperity. I try to get their eyes off of the problem and on the solution. Over and over people tell me exactly what they owe, exactly when the money is due and exactly what will happen to them if they don't pay. Over and over I reply to them with promises from the Word of God. I continually urge them to at least give "equal time" to the solution—to spend at least as much time focusing on the solutions in God's Word as they do in focusing on every last detail of the financial bondage that they are in. God's laws of prosperity do work. If people aren't so bound up with fear as a result of their financial problems that they reject the teachings of God, these teachings will show them the way out of their financial prison.

In the world, people study *The Wall Street Journal* and all the stock market tips to decide how to handle their money. This is fine for man's system of prosperity, but Christians should study God's laws of prosperity which are found in the greatest instruction book that this world has ever known— the Holy Bible.

Tithes and offerings are better than any investment that this world has ever seen. God's laws of tithing and giving are much more precise and exact than the world's laws of finance. If we'll pay the price of following God's laws of prosperity, no financial problem on the face of this earth will be able to defeat us.

Chapter Twelve

We Can't Outgive God

Now we are ready to see what God's Word has to say about the subject of giving. Sowing and reaping, tithing and giving all overlap in some areas, but in each area there is a wealth of new scriptural teaching which is not covered in the other areas.

God's Word teaches that all giving should be based upon love. "If I gave everything I have to poor people, and if I were buried alive for preaching the gospel but didn't love others, it would be of no value whatever" (I Corinthians 13:3 *The Living Bible*). Some people learn part of God's laws of prosperity and give in a calculating manner, anticipating something in return. This won't work! Giving without love is *"of no value whatever."* No matter what we give, if our gift isn't based upon love, it is worth nothing. Love is the key to giving and only love opens the channels for our loving Father to give back to us.

Our Father has given us very definite laws for giving and receiving. Let's start with the foundation verse of scripture on this and expand from there. "Give, and it shall be given unto you; good measure, pressed down, and shaken together, and running over, shall men give into your bosom. For with the same measure that ye mete withal it shall be measured unto you again" (Luke 6:38).

There is a tremendous depth of meaning in this one verse of scripture. Let's take it apart piece by piece. This verse starts by simply telling us that if we give, we will receive in return. This ties in exactly with ". . . whatsoever a man soweth, that shall he also reap" (Galatians 6:7) which we covered in our study on sowing and reaping. Giving is a seed and, if we sow it properly, God will see that we receive a harvest.

The Living Bible explains this part of Luke 6:38 beautifully. ". . . Your gift will return to you in full and overflowing measure, pressed down, shaken together to make room for more, and running over . . ." *We can't outgive God!* When we give according to God's laws, our gift will come back to us overflowing and running over.

Imagine a large container of oats. Before we receive from these oats they will be "pressed down" so they settle into the bottom of the container, enabling more oats to be added. Then these oats will be "shaken together" so that they will settle down even more, enabling still more oats to be added. When all this process is completed, the container will be filled to overflowing. It will be so full that oats will be "running over" the sides. *This is how God's Word tells us that we will receive if we give freely according to His laws of giving.

This ties in with Malachi 3:10 which tells us that, if we give properly of our tithes and offerings, God will open up the windows of heaven and pour out blessings that will be so great that we won't have room to receive them. God clearly promises to give back all that we give . . . and much, much more.

How will God give back to us? Will He just pour money down from heaven? No, Luke 6:38 tells us that "men" will give unto us. ". . . shall *men* give unto your bosom . . ." What does this mean? It means that our Father has arranged it so that His children who follow His laws of giving will receive— from men. As we give generously to others, our Father will inspire other men and women to give to us.

This giving can be in many forms. We might receive an especially good deal in business. Or, we might buy or sell a home, a car or some other property in a manner that is very favorable to us. If we are self-employed, people might be led to do business with us. If we are employed, our employer may be led to give us a promotion, a pay raise or a bonus. Or, we might be offered a new job that is much better than the one we have. These are just a few of the numerous ways that our Father can use to cause other men to give to us.

What part do we play in getting other people to give to us? As we have seen, God's Word tells us that this is accomplished by constantly giving to others. ". . . all things whatsoever ye would that men should do to you, do ye even so to them: for this is the law . . ." (Matthew 7:12). Whatever we want to reap, we first must sow. This is God's law.

We determine exactly how much others give to us. How do we do this? The closing words of Luke 6:38 tell us how. ". . . for with the same measure that ye mete withal it shall be measured to you

113

again." Thus, if we give with a teaspoon, we will receive "teaspoon measure" in return. If we give with a tablespoon, we will receive in "tablespoon measure." If we give by the barrel, we will receive "by the barrel." Whatever measure we use to give is exactly what will be used to measure what is given back to us.

The principles of Luke 6:38 apply to every area of our lives—including our finances. The giving of our money is very important to God because most of the money and possessions that we have were earned by giving of ourselves—our abilities, our energy and our time. When we understand this concept, we can see how our employment is actually a vehicle that we use to turn ourselves into dollars that can be invested in God's work as He leads us to give them. ". . . let him labour, working with his hands the thing which is good, that he may have to give to him that needeth" (Ephesians 4:28).

Next, let's look at nine words that Jesus Christ said—words which virtually every reader of this book has heard before. "It is more blessed to give than to receive" (Acts 20:35). Many of us have heard these words many times and many of us think that we agree with these words. However, in many cases, I honestly don't believe this is the case. I believe that most people place a lot more emphasis on "getting" than they do on giving.

Be completely honest. *Do you* honestly get a lot more enjoyment out of giving than you do out of receiving? Our Father knows us as we really are. I believe that, as He looks at what most of us are like deep down inside of our hearts, He sees that many of His children place much more emphasis on receiving than they do on giving.

114

However, His Word clearly teaches that He put us on this earth not to see how much we can get, but to see how much we can give. Untold millions of people have this backwards. When we are reborn spiritually, our new nature wants to give, but our old nature wants to hang on to what we have. Jesus tells us that it is more blessed to give than it is to receive. He wouldn't have said this if it wasn't true. Why is it more blessed to give than it is to receive? I can think of four reasons:

(1) When we give freely and generously, we put God first ahead of our own selfish interests. By doing this, we are obeying His Word and this obedience will cause Him to bless us.

(2) When we give freely and generously, this shows that we trust God. The degree of our giving is a clear indication of our freedom from fear. Freedom from fear is always a blessing.

(3) When we give freely and generously, this protects us from the pitfalls of greed and covetousness. Generous giving comes from a humble loving heart. Greed and selfishness are derived from a prideful "me first" heart and this blocks us from the blessings of God. ". . . God resisteth the proud, and giveth grace to the humble" (I Peter 5:5).

(4) Finally, we are blessed because, the more we give to God, the more this opens the channel for Him to see that we receive abundantly in return. If we withhold our giving, we are actually withholding the blessing that our Father wants to give us. The "receiving" that most people want deep down in their hearts actually comes as a result of our giving. This is one reason why Jesus said that it is more blessed to give than it is to receive because, by our giving, we do receive.

When we manage to grasp these principles, giving really does become a blessing. In fact, we will get to the point where, when we give a little, it hurts and when we give a great deal it doesn't hurt at all. This will sound strange to you if you haven't given much, but Christians who have given freely on many occasions will agree to the absolute truth of this statement.

Our Father doesn't want us to give because we think that we "have to"—because we feel that it is an obligation. He wants us to give cheerfully. "Every man according as he purposeth in his heart, so let him give; not grudgingly, or of necessity: for God loveth a cheerful giver" (II Corinthians 9:7).

God's Word tells us that He doesn't want us to give grudgingly because we feel that this is a necessity. Yet, this is exactly the way that many people give to God. They give out of fear—through a sense of duty. They dole out the dollars carefully and begrudge what they do give. God didn't give us His Son grudgingly. Jesus didn't give His life grudgingly on the cross. He gladly paid the debt for every one of the sins ever committed by every person who will ever live on this earth. None of us could even begin to repay Jesus for what He did for us if we had trillions of dollars and gave it all to Him.

It's interesting to study the Greek word that is translated *cheerful* in II Corinthians 9:7. This Greek word is *hilares* which means *noisy and full of fun and laughter. This* is how God wants us to give! Instead of giving grudgingly, He wants us to be excited. He wants us to have fun giving. I ask you, does the word *hilarious* describe your giving?? Or,

116

does the first part of this verse of scripture describe your giving—"grudgingly . . .or of necessity??"

If we observe the people in a typical church service as the collection plate is passed, how often do we see people who are excited about their giving—giving laughingly and happily? In the church that I belong to, we sometimes applaud when we give our offerings. I believe we should do this all the time. If we really understand God's laws of prosperity, our time of giving will always be a time of cheerful rejoicing.

Too many Christians look upon their giving as an obligation that they owe instead of as a seed that they sow. The times when we give should be the greatest times of our lives. As always, this is completely opposite to the world's way—most people think that the times that they "get" are the happiest times of their lives.

Why shouldn't we give cheerfully if we *know* that our money is going to be put to good use and, in addition if we *know* that God is going to see to it that every bit of our gift is given back to us plus more? Who wouldn't be cheerful if they fully comprehended that, in addition to doing God's work, they would receive a bountiful harvest from the seeds that they had sown??

God blesses the cheerful giver—not the grudging giver. If you go down to the bank and put money in a savings account, do you do it cheerfully or grudgingly? When we put our money in the Bank of Heaven we put our money in a bank that is greater than any bank that this world has ever known. We put our money in a bank that has a better guarantee than any bank in this world.

117

Our "savings account" in the Bank of Heaven is backed by the Word of God. Can we believe Him? God's Word tells us over and over that, if we give bountifully, we will receive bountifully in return. When we fully comprehend this and believe this with all our hearts, we'll be very, very cheerful when we give.

Chapter Thirteen

Giving God's Way

Our Father's Word gives us specific instructions as to exactly how He wants us to live our lives. He blesses us in exact proportion to what His Word tells us to do.

One thing that God's Word clearly tells us to do is to give to the poor. When we have a financial need in our lives, I believe that God often arranges so that someone with worse needs comes across our path. Despite problems with our own finances, we can reach out and help that person if we really want to.

Do we?? If we do, we plant the seeds which enable God to solve our larger financial problems. If we don't, we fail to plant the seeds that God was looking for so that He could provide the necessary harvest to meet our own financial needs. "Blessed is he that considereth the poor; the Lord will deliver him in time of trouble. The Lord will preserve him, and keep him alive; and he shall be blessed upon the earth" (Psalm 41:1-2).

When the poor people cross our path, we shouldn't turn away from them. If we give to them, we will be blessed and we will never lack. "He that hath a bountiful eye shall be blessed; for he giveth of his bread to the poor" (Proverbs 22:9). "He that giveth unto the poor shall not lack: but he that hideth his eyes shall have many a curse" (Proverbs 28:27).

God's Word tells us that, as we reach out to help the hungry and those who are in trouble, this will bring the light of God into our lives. When we do this, the Lord will guide us continually and supply us with all good things—including good health. "Feed the hungry! Help those in trouble! Then your light will shine out from the darkness, and the darkness around you shall be bright as day. And the Lord will guide you continually, and satisfy you with all good things, and keep you healthy, too, and you will be like a well-watered garden, like an ever-flowing spring" (Isaiah 58:10-11 *The Living Bible*).

God's Word tells us that, when we give to the poor, we are actually lending to Him—and that He will pay us back. How can we lend money to anyone with better credit than God? He has the best credit rating in the entire universe! This is a loan with a guaranteed return and we know that our Father pays abundant rates of interest. "He that hath pity unto the poor lendeth unto the Lord; and that which he hath given will he pay him again" (Proverbs 19:17).

I'm not saying that we should give money to every "down and outer" in the world. Many times this will hurt them more than it will help them. God doesn't want us to be a "soft touch" for everyone with a "sob story." We should seek the Lord's will before giving or lending money. "A good man sheweth favor and lendeth: he will guide his affairs with discretion" (Psalm 112:5).

When we give money to the poor, we actually receive a two-fold blessing. First, we know that the money we give is helping people who desperately need help and we know this is the Lord's wish. "Bear ye one another's burdens, and so fulfill the law of Christ" (Galatians 6:2). Second, we're not actually "spending" anything when we do this— we're sowing seeds which will produce a harvest (Galatians 6:7).

If we really comprehend these principles, we'll give freely to help the poor of the world. As the Lord continues to give back to us, we'll continue to give more and more freely. This won't cost us one cent. The Lord wants to use our faith as a channel through which He can and will pour large amounts of money to fulfill His great commission throughout the world.

We can help poor people tremendously by giving to them, but we can help them even more by teaching them how to apply God's laws of prosperity in their own lives. An old saying says, "If you give a man a fish, you give him one meal, but if you teach him how to fish, you show him how to get food for the rest of his life."

When I came to the Lord, I was poor. I was in a seemingly hopeless financial situation with an annual debt repayment schedule that was more than my annual income. However, I gave my life to Jesus Christ and I began to study and meditate in God's Word day and night, learning everything that I could about God's laws of prosperity.

As I studied and meditated for tremendous long hours, I learned from the Bible that people who are in debt can, (a) meditate their way out of debt (Psalm 1:1-3; Joshua 1:8). and, (b) give their way out of debt (Luke 6:38, II Corinthians 9:6-8 and Malachi 3:8-11). After many months of darkness, I finally "saw a light at the end of the tunnel."

It's not easy to give when our debts are large, yet this is exactly what we must do. We can give (and meditate) our way out of debt. I know. I did it. I have seen many other people do it. This sounds incongruous to anyone whose mind has not been renewed, but it is a fact that is backed solidly by the Word of God.

Am I saying that, if someone is really "down and out," that he should start giving freely to God? This is exactly what I'm saying. Many Christian missionaries have testified about how they went into poverty-stricken countries and taught God's laws of giving to the people there and saw God bless them abundantly. If God's laws of giving will work in the underdeveloped, poverty-stricken nations of the world, they certainly will work in the United States and other countries with a much higher standard of living.

When I first started counseling with other Christians on this subject, I used to tell people with financial problems that I thought God would forgive them because they just didn't have enough to give. This was wrong. I never counsel this way now. If we tell people that they shouldn't give, we're really cheating them out of a harvest which they can't receive unless they plant their seeds.

There are many good Christian books which tell people how to get out of debt, how to manage their budgets, how to stretch their dollars, etc. I have read several of these books and some of them are full of good logical, practical advice. However, I have never yet read one that even comes close to putting the proper emphasis on continual giving and constant meditation ahead of everything else. This is what God's Word teaches and we must follow His instructions.

Jesus pointed out the importance of giving when it seems as though we can't give. "Then He went over to the collection boxes in the temple and sat and watched as the crowds dropped in their money. Some who were rich put in large amounts. Then a poor widow came and dropped in two pennies. He called His disciples to Him and remarked, "That widow has given more than all those rich men put together! For they gave a little of their extra fat, while she gave up her last penny" (Mark 12:41-44 *The Living Bible*).

The dollar amount that we give isn't as important as the proportion that we give compared to what we are able to give. ". . . if the (eager) readiness to give is there, then it is acceptable and welcomed in proportion to what a person has, not according to what he does not have" (II Corinthians 8:12 *The Amplified Bible*).

Many people give faithfully for awhile and then, when financial problems come up, they cut down on their giving. If we fall into this trap, we fail a financial test that God has allowed to come into our lives. When financial problems come, if we make *any* change in our giving, it should be to *increase* our giving, not to decrease it. In times of difficulty, it's more important than ever to put God first and to keep Him first. We certainly aren't doing this if we cut down on our giving.

Nine years ago, when my world was falling apart emotionally and financially, I learned "the twin towers of strength" from the fourth chapter of Philippians: Philippians 4:19, "But my God shall supply all your needs according to his riches in glory by Christ Jesus" and Philippians 4:13, "I can do all things through Christ which strengtheneth me." These two verses of scripture picked me up off the floor many, many times.

All over the world Christians are boldly claiming the harvest of Philippians 4:19. I'm not saying that it is wrong to say that God will supply all of our needs, but I do know that God will do His part to the degree that we do our part. We should be careful about expecting to reap the harvest of Philippians 4:19 without first of all planting the seeds of Philippians 4:15-18.

In Philippians 4:15 Paul says that, when he left Macedonia, only one church gave to his ministry—the Philippian church. In verse 16, Paul says that when he was in Thessalonica the Philippians again gave to him when he was in need. In verse 17, Paul tells the Philippians that their giving has caused fruit to "abound" to their "account." In verse 18 he tells them that God is well pleased with the sacrifices that they have made.

It was only *after* he made these statements that Paul made the famous statement about God supplying all of our needs according to His riches in glory by Christ Jesus. I believe that the promise of Philippians 4:19 is the harvest and I believe that this harvest is based upon the seeds that were planted in Philippians 4:15-18.

God's Word tells the Philippians that He will supply all of their needs for the same reason that He will supply all of our needs—*because* they gave freely. If we have sowed the seeds of giving, this verse of scripture tells us that God Himself will supply all of our needs. He is our source—not our jobs, our savings accounts or anything else. If we have given properly, we are told that our needs will be met from God's riches.

Another important law of giving is God's law of quiet giving. We should never give so that other people will know what we have given. Some people want recognition for being great givers. The Scriptures warn us against this. "Take care! Don't do your good deeds publicly, to be admired, for then you will lose the reward from your Father in heaven. When you give a gift to a beggar, don't shout about it as the hypocrites do—blowing trumpets in the synagogues and streets to call attention to their acts of charity! I tell you in all earnestness, they have received all the reward they will ever get. But when you do a kindness to someone, do it secretly—don't tell your left hand what your right hand is doing. And your Father who knows all secrets will reward you" (Matthew 6:1-4 *The Living Bible*).

If we look for others to admire us because of what we have given, their recognition will be our only reward. If we give quietly and without fanfare, our Father in heaven will know about it and He will reward us.

Our Father wants us to give wisely. We should be very careful where we plant our seeds just as farmers are careful where they plant seeds. If they don't plant seeds in fertile soil, they often won't grow. Or, if they do grow, they won't produce much of a harvest. Luke 8:5-8 tells us about the sower who sowed seed by the wayside, on a rock, among thorns and on good ground. Only the seed that fell on good ground took root and sprung up and produced a bountiful harvest.

This is true in the agricultural realm and it's also true in the spiritual realm. When we plant our financial seeds, I believe that it is very important for us to prayerfully ask where we should plant them. We should always seek the Lord's will before we give. Luke 6:38 tells us that the Lord uses men to give to other men. He might very well intend to use us to give to a specific person or organization and this is one reason why it is always important for us to seek His will before we give.

As mentioned earlier, I believe that our tithes should go to the local church—the storehouse . . . the place where we are fed spiritually on a regular basis throughout the year. However, our offerings can go to any number of different places. Often, it's not easy to decide on this. Christians often find themselves besieged with requests from many different Christian ministries.

Our Father doesn't want us to complicate our giving. He wants us to keep it simple. ". . . he that giveth, let him do it with simplicity . . ." (Romans 12:8). When we're besieged with requests to give to Christian television programs, radio programs and to many Christian organizations which contact us through the mail, God doesn't want us to be confused. "For God is not the author of confusion, but of peace . . ." (I Corinthians 14:33).

I used to be frustrated by all of the requests that I got to give, but I don't get frustrated now. When I wonder if the Lord wants me to give to a particular ministry, I ask Him in prayer. As the years have gone by, I have learned to give more and more as God's Holy Spirit leads me to give and less and less as an emotional response to the barrage of requests

126

from many seemingly good Christian causes. Now I give as I am led to give. However, I lay my hands on every request that I receive and I pray for that organization.

I also believe that Christians should plan to continue serving the Lord financially after they have died and gone to heaven. I believe that all of us should make provisions for our families after we die. I have done this with life insurance. I also have arranged my life insurance so that part of it will be used after I die to continue to give money that I very definitely would have given if I had lived.

We should be careful about leaving "our" money so that it will be squabbled over after our death and perhaps not used for the purposes that the Lord would want it used for. How many Christians, as a result of improper financial planning, have allowed "their" money to be used after death for purposes that they would not have agreed to while they were still alive? We must not allow this to happen.

Chapter Fourteen

God's Laws of Receiving

$\mathbf{W}$e have studied God's laws of giving in detail. Now it is time to study God's laws of receiving. Many Christians have learned how to give, but they don't know how to receive. Receiving also isn't "automatic." When we give, God doesn't automatically rain blessings down from the skies. If we want to receive from God, it is our duty to find His laws of receiving in His Word and then to study and meditate on them and apply them in our lives.

Let's review the receiving end of some of God's promises that we have discussed in our previous chapters. Luke 6:38 tells us that we can receive in "good measure, pressed down, and shaken together, and running over." II Corinthians 9:6 tells us that we can "reap bountifully." Malachi 3:10 tells us that God will open up the windows of heaven and pour out such a great blessing "that there shall not be room enough to receive it."

Many Christians are receiving only a "trickle" of God's promised blessings instead of the overflowing abundance that is promised by His Word. Why is this? I believe that the reason is that many Christians know and apply God's laws of giving, but they don't know and apply His laws of receiving.

Are you planting ample financial seeds and failing to receive abundantly? If so, God tells us what we should do. ". . . Consider your ways, Ye have sown much, and bring in little; ye eat, but ye have not enough; ye drink, but ye are not filled with drink; ye clothe you, but there is none warm; and he that earneth wages earneth wages to put it into a bag with holes. Thus saith the Lord of hosts; Consider your ways" (Haggai 1:6-7).

God's Word clearly speaks of people who "have sown much, and bring in little." Therefore, an abundant return obviously isn't automatic. We *don't* "automatically" receive bountifully just because we sow bountifully. If we're sowing abundantly and not receiving abundantly, what does God's Word tell us to do? Our Father tells us twice to "consider your ways." He is actually telling us that we need to take a good look at what we're doing if we're sowing seeds bountifully and if we're still not receiving bountifully.

So, let's take a good look at exactly what we should do after we sow our financial seeds. What does a farmer do after he sows his seeds? Does he just sow the seeds and then forget about them? If he does, he isn't going to receive a very good harvest. The successful farmer does a lot more than that. After the seeds are sown, he cultivates the crop. He puts fertilizer on it. He sees that it receives enough water. He clears out weeds. The return from seeds can vary greatly. It all depends upon how good the soil is and how effectively it is cultivated if the seeds are to produce a maximum harvest.

The same principles apply in the financial realm. After planting our financial seeds, we must cultivate them. We must continue to study and meditate constantly in God's Word. We must constantly express our faith in an abundant return by our words and our actions. No matter how bad a situation might appear, we must not block God in any way by lack of faith . . . or by lack of patience.

Lack of patience blocks more Christians from receiving from God than many of us realize. A farmer wouldn't dream of planting seeds and expecting an immediate harvest. We can't rush this process. God's laws of sowing and reaping always take time. God has a time for everything. "To every thing there is a season, and a time to every purpose under the heaven . . ." (Ecclesiastes 3:1). It takes a certain amount of time to grow tomatoes. It takes a certain amount of time to grow corn. It takes approximately nine months for a woman to have a baby.

God's Word says, "Cast thy bread upon the waters: for thou shalt find it *after many days*" (Ecclesiastes 11:1). The word *bread* means anything of substance to us—our money, our time, our abilities, etc. The word *waters* refers to people who have needs. The first part of this verse of scripture tells us, "Give your money, your time and your abilities to people who have need of them. The second part of this verse of scripture says that God will give back to us when His time is right—not ours. We will receive our harvest "after many days." Many of us are expecting a return when our seeds haven't had time to take root and grow and produce a harvest.

Our Father tells us in III John 2 that He wants very much for us to prosper "even as thy soul prospereth." This shows us that the key to God's prosperity is in our souls. Jesus told us, "In your patience possess ye your souls" (Luke 21:19). If we are to prosper under God's laws of prosperity, we must be patient. God doesn't lie. All of His promises are real. We will reap—if we are patient. We can't rush God. The carnal part of us wants answers and it wants them now! We must counteract this tendency by developing ourselves spiritually so that we will have the strength and the patience to wait for the harvest. "And let us not be weary in well-doing: for in due season we shall reap, if we faint not" (Galatians 6:9).

Reaping is not "automatic." God's Word tells us that we will reap "if." In other words, the reaping is conditional. It is conditional upon our patience. It depends on whether or not we get tired of waiting and give up. If we do, we negate God's promises of reaping.

Faith and patience go together. The Book of Hebrews has a lot to say about the subject of faith and, on at least three occasions, faith is tied into patience. ". . . be not slothful, but followers of them who *through faith and patience* inherit the promises (Hebrews 6:12). We won't receive bountiful returns if we are "slothful"—if we are lazy and unwilling to pay the price. We must show both faith and patience if we expect to receive from God. ". . . *after he had patiently endured*, he obtained the promise" (Hebrews 6:15).

Receiving from God isn't "automatic." We must work hard studying and meditating in God's Word if we expect to develop our faith to the point where we will receive blessings from Him. We must be certain that we don't throw away our confidence in God because of lack of patience. "For ye have need of *patience*, that after ye have done the will of God, ye might receive the promise" (Hebrews 10:36).

We develop this patience by trusting in God's Holy Spirit within us. If we really do this, patience is just one of the fruits that we will receive. ". . . when the Holy Spirit controls our lives He will produce this kind of fruit in us: love, joy, peace, *patience* kindness, goodness, faithfulness, gentleness and self-control . . ." (Galatians 5:22-23 *The Living Bible*).

Our Father wants us to be single-minded. Our faith must be firm. If we don't get a prompt answer, we must not begin to wonder and doubt. ". . . ask in faith, nothing wavering. For he that wavereth is like a wave of the sea driven with the wind and tossed. For let not that man think that he shall receive any thing of the Lord. A double-minded man is unstable in all his ways" (James 1:6-8).

Wavering indicates unbelief. Wavering shows that we really don't expect to receive from God. I have studied God's laws of prosperity for many years and I know them well. Nevertheless, I still experience seasons of financial difficulty. When this happens, I don't waver in the least. Instead, I have learned to meditate and study even more and to show my faith by increasing my giving.

When everything looks bad, I have learned to open my mouth and confess that God will provide abundantly just as He has promised. ". . . let us seize and hold fast and retain without wavering the hope we cherish and confess, and our acknowledgement of it, for He who promised is reliable (sure) and faithful to His word" (Hebrews 10:23 *Amplified Bible*).

132

If we aren't receiving an answer, we need to speak out the promises of Joshua 1:8, Psalm 1:1-3, Malachi 3:10-11, Luke 6:38, II Corinthians 9:6-8 and many others. We need to praise God and thank Him for supplying abundantly. We must "stick to our guns." Too many Christians waver after awhile and allow their doubts to come out of their mouths. This negative confession cancels the results that would have been forthcoming if they had continued to cultivate their crops with faith and patience.

We must not doubt God's Word. Our words and our actions should constantly show our faith in the promises of God. We should boldly claim the return from our tithes and offerings. We should boldly say, "I have given freely and, because I have given freely, my Father gives back to me. You say this in your Word, Father, and in Jesus' name, I thank you for this return."

The farmer has to clear out the weeds in his garden. We clear out weeds in the spiritual realm by boldly confessing the promises of God in spite of the weeds that are trying to choke off our harvest. If we really do believe that we're going to receive from God, we should talk and act exactly the way we would talk and act if we had a guaranteed Certificate of Deposit that we know would mature in time to meet all of our needs! God's Word is a much stronger assurance than any worldly promise to pay.

We see this clearly in the example of Jesus Christ. Jesus just "knew" that the bread and fish would be there when He had to feed the multitude. He "knew" that the coin would be inside of the mouth of the fish when money was needed to pay taxes. He "knew" that the net would come up full when He told the fishermen to put it down after a night of fruitless fishing.

This *same* certainty of God's provision is available to us today. We have all the Old Testament promises that Jesus had plus all of the New Testament promises. The *same* Holy Sprit who lived inside of Jesus Christ two thousand years ago lives inside us today. He is just as willing and just as able to provide abundantly today as He was then. The *only* variable is the faith and patience of Jesus compared with the faith and patience that you and I exhibit today.

While we're waiting for our "crop" to come in, we must cultivate it by continuing to believe and by continually confessing the promises of God. We need to "water" our seeds with constant, unwavering faith and patience, refusing to let the "weeds" of doubt and discouragement choke off our harvest.

Our Father doesn't want us to limit Him in any way. He knows no limits. The only limits are those that we impose through lack of belief in His promises. ". . . *if* thou canst believe, *all* things are possible to him that believeth . . ." (Mark 9:23). However, we can block Him through lack of faith on our part. Our Father has given us complete freedom of choice and He's not going to force Himself upon us. He'll act according to our faith.

If our doubtful words and actions show that we don't believe that we'll receive from Him, our lack of faith blocks Him from providing abundantly for us as He wants so very much to do. Our Father will bless us. We will receive from Him—in exact proportion to our unwavering belief that we will receive. This is His law.

We must be open and receptive to God's promises. We should always expect to receive. Constant faith enables our Father to give much more abundantly to us. Every Christian should want to receive—*not* just for his own needs, but as a channel for God to use to meet the needs of others. Even when we're prosperous, we must be willing to be used as a channel so God can bless others through us.

There isn't anything wrong with expecting to receive from God. Many people fail to receive from God because they think it's wrong to believe for a return from their giving. *Where* in God's Word does it say that??? Virtually every one of God's instructions on giving is combined with a promise of receiving. See for yourself in Luke 6:38, II Corinthians 9:6-8, Malachi 3:10-11, etc. If God Himself places an emphasis on receiving, *why* should we feel that there is anything wrong with expecting to receive???

We should expect a return on our giving. All Christians should release their faith for a great return, not to "feather their own nests," but to finance world-wide Christian revival. This is the primary reason why all Christians should learn and apply God's laws of receiving. There is absolutely nothing wrong with "giving to get" if the purpose of the "getting" is to spread the gospel of Jesus Christ throughout the world! Instead of being wrong, it is our obligation to learn exactly how to "give to get" and to act in faith upon what we have learned.

It's wrong to give selfishly, but it's not wrong to give believing. Money that is constantly given is like a clear, bubbling brook—always fresh and new, always cool and refreshing. This continual giving, backed up by unwavering faith and patience, will continually activate God's laws of receiving and put us in His perfect will for our finances.

Chapter Fifteen

God's Laws Of
Banking and Investment

In the previous fourteen chapters, we have touched all of the bases. We have talked about why God wants us to prosper and how to prosper by following God's laws of renewal, study and meditation, belief, confession and obedience. We have discussed God's laws of sowing and reaping, His laws of tithing and giving and His laws of receiving.

Now we're ready to pull all of this together as we look at God's laws of banking and investment. We're going to talk about a bank that most financial experts on this earth have never heard of—the Bank of Heaven. We're going to talk about investments that never have been listed on the New York Stock Exchange.

God's banking and investment laws are very different from the world's banking and investment laws. The primary difference is that the banking and investing that we do in the world's system will benefit us only during our lifetime on this earth. The banking and investment laws that we'll discuss in this chapter will also benefit us during this lifetime, but much more important, these transactions will also benefit all Christians for the endless years of eternity that we'll spend together in heaven.

Every dollar that we spend on ourselves here on this earth perishes as we spend it. However, every dollar that we give to God while we are on this earth is deposited to our accounts in the Bank of Heaven—accounts which can be used while we are on this earth and accounts which also will be available to all Christians for eternity.

When we give money to God, it is deposited in His bank—a bank from which our funds can't be stolen, a bank where our funds won't be affected at all by worldly economic conditions and a bank that pays interest rates which are beyond our human conception.

Every reader who understands God's laws of banking and investment will revolutionize his financial thinking. If you realize that God has a separate set of financial laws that transcend the earthly realm, you'll spend hours and hours studying and meditating on God's laws of prosperity in order to learn everything that you possibly can about how they work.

Just think how we could transform this world if, by learning and applying God's laws of prosperity, millions of Christians gave hundreds of billions of dollars to God's work here on this earth. Instead of being spent on temporary, worldly pleasures, this money would be used for eternal, spiritual purposes. God's laws are exactly the opposite from the way that we think with our carnal worldly minds.

God's laws say, "The only thing that you will get to keep are the things that you give away." If we follow God's laws of prosperity, every one of our needs will be met while we're here on this earth and we'll have plenty left over to give away (II

Corinthians 9:6-8). If we give this money away as God leads us to give it, every bit of this money will be deposited into our accounts in the Bank of Heaven. "Jesus said unto him, if thou wilt be perfect, go and sell what thou hast, and give to the poor and thou shalt have treasure in heaven . . ." (Matthew 19:21).

God's Word tells us that He wants us to use our money on this earth to help others. "Tell them to use their money to do good. They should be rich in good works and should give happily to those in need, always being ready to share with others whatever God has given them. By doing this they will be storing up real treasure for themselves in heaven—it is the only safe investment for eternity! And they will be living a fruitful Christian life down here as well" (I Timothy 6:18-19 *The Living Bible*).

We instinctively want to "store up" treasure and this is fine with God as long as we store it up in the right place. Instead of hanging tightly onto "our" money here on this earth, our Father wants us to give it away freely and cheerfully. We will lay up treasure in heaven in exact proportion to the degree that we give freely to others of ourselves and "our" money while we live on this earth.

Jesus emphatically warned us of the dangers of storing up money here on this earth. He said, "Lay not up for yourselves treasures upon earth, where moth and rust doth corrupt and where thieves break through and steal: but lay up for yourselves treasures in heaven, where neither moth nor rust doth corrupt, and where thieves do not break through nor steal: For where your treasure is, there will your heart be also" (Matthew 6:19-21).

139

I believe that the "moth" and "rust" and "corruption" that Jesus speaks about are the inflation, the high interest rates and the selfish tendencies of the world's economic system. These cruel and negative influences are destroying the life savings of people who have depended upon them.

Who are the "thieves" that Jesus said will break through and steal the money that we store up on earth? The answer is obvious—God's Word tells us that these thieves are Satan and his evil spirits. "The *thief* cometh not, but for to steal, and to kill and to destroy . . ." (John 10:10). Satan is a thief and he'll steal from us in every way that he can while we're here on earth. Two of his favorite devices are to try to influence us to spend "our" money on selfish desires or to store it up to provide ourselves with worldly security.

Satan can't steal what we have deposited in the Bank of Heaven because he can't get at it. Inflation, high interest rates and other economic uncertainties that plague savings accounts here on earth have no effect whatever on the Bank of Heaven. In I Timothy 6:7, we are warned against trusting in "uncertain" riches. This refers to the riches of this world which are subject to the ravages of inflation, recession and unemployment. Instead, God wants us to trust in our "certain riches"—the riches that we have on deposit with Him.

Have you given freely to God for many years? If so, then you have a sizable account in the Bank of Heaven. If not, it isn't too late. Now is the time to start following God's laws of prosperity with a definite program of tithes and offerings. As our worldly economy gets worse and worse, this will be more important because God's laws will provide for us during the remainder of our lives on earth and also throughout our eternal lives in heaven.

There isn't anything wrong with setting money aside for a "rainy day" as long as we put it in the right bank! If and when the stock market fails or inflation goes wild or anything else happens to cause our man-made economic system to crumble, our money will still be there in the Bank of Heaven—untouched by any of the calamities of the world's economic system.

We are able to open accounts in the Bank of Heaven when we are in good standing with this bank based upon the reference of Jesus Christ. We receive this good standing by accepting Him as our Lord and Saviour. This enables us to obtain a passbook in the Bank of Heaven.

We make deposits and withdrawals in this account following God's laws of banking. The Bank of Heaven has definite laws just as banks on earth have laws that they operate by. We can't conduct transactions in a bank on earth unless we follow its procedures. The Bank of Heaven is no different. We must follow God's laws of banking to put money into His bank and we must follow His laws of banking to get money out of His bank. These laws are clearly spelled out in His Book of Instructions— the Holy Bible.

If we have given freely of our money here on this earth, we can go to the Bank of Heaven whenever we need to make a withdrawal. None of us would hesitate to make a withdrawal from a bank here on earth where we had money on deposit. We'd go to that bank with complete confidence. It's no different when we do business with the Bank of Heaven.

As long as we have made our deposits through tithes and offerings, the money is available to us. How do we get this money out of our account in the Bank of Heaven? We do it by releasing our faith—by presenting our "faith check" to the Bank of Heaven.

We do this first of all by going to this bank in Jesus' Name—this is the key that opens the door to our heavenly account. We then tell our Father that we need a certain amount of money and we request this amount with the same faith and confidence that we would have if we requested a withdrawal from a worldly bank. We withdraw our money from the Bank of Heaven by faith. Our withdrawal request will be honored to the exact degree of our faith. Many people never make this request. ". . . ye have not, because ye ask not" (James 4:2).

God's laws of banking tell us that we *won't* be able to withdraw money from the Bank of Heaven for selfish reasons. "Ye ask and receive not, because ye ask amiss, that ye may consume it upon your lusts" (James 4:3). If we need to withdraw from that heavenly account, we can as long as our prayer—our request for withdrawal—is in line with God's will for our lives. When we ask according to God's will (His laws), He will hear our request and He will grant our request. "And this is the confidence that we have in him, that, if we ask *any* thing *according to his will,* he heareth us: and if we *know* that he *hear* us, whatsoever we ask, we *know* that we *have* the petitions that we desired of him" (I John 5:14-15).

In fact, God's Word tells us that we can make withdrawals from our heavenly acounts in an amount equal to one hundred times the amount

142

that we have deposited! God's Word tells us that we can make this hundredfold withdrawal now—at this time—here on earth. "And, Jesus answered and said, Verily I say unto you, There is no man that hath left house, or brethren, or sisters, or father, or mother, or wife, or children, or lands, for my sake, and the gospel's, but he shall receive an hundredfold *now in this time*, houses and brethren, and sisters, and mothers, and children, and lands, with persecutions; and in the world to come eternal life" (Mark 10:29-30).

These are some of the most important and also some of the most misunderstood words in the entire Bible. Exactly what is Jesus saying to us? First, we should define what a "hundredfold" return is. If you give $1,000 to the Lord and He provides a hundredfold return on this money, how much will you get back? Does this mean you will get back twice as much—$2,000 for every $1,000?? . . . ten times as much—$10,000 for every $1,000?? . . . or, one hundred times as much—$100,000 for every $1,000??

God's Word says that He will give us back $100,00 for every $1,000 that we give—one hundred times as much as we give. This is absolutely awesome when it is compared with the world's interest rates. This is a 10,000% return! When will God give us this return? Does this refer to heaven? No. Mark 10:30 clearly says "now in this time." There is no question whatever that God's Word clearly says that we can receive a "hundredfold" return "now in this time."

This statement has caused some of the most misguided teaching in the entire Bible. Some people are giving money to the Lord and then they are boldly claiming a hundredfold return for selfish, lustful reasons. This is completely wrong. The hundredfold return *is* available to us in this lifetime, but *not* for selfish, lustful purposes. This hundredfold return is very rare. Only a select few people have ever qualified for it. Let me prove this to you. Do you know or have you even heard of anyone who has received back $100,000 in this lifetime for every $1,000 that they have given to the Lord?? Do you know anyone who has even come close to receiving this return?? Many Christians are going around boldly claiming this return, but the truth is that they have never received a return even close to this amount nor do they know anyone who has!

There is a great deal of confusion about the hundredfold return. In fact, as we have already seen, in Mark 10:25 Jesus said "It is easier for a camel to go through the eye of a needle than for a rich man to enter into the kingdom of God." Then, in almost the same breath (in Mark 10:30), Jesus told His disciples that they could receive a hundredfold return here on this earth and also enjoy eternal life with Him in the world to come.

How can we explain this? Don't these statements seem to contradict one another? There is a clear explanation. *If* we qualify, God will give a 10,000% return to us right here on this earth. What must we do in order to qualify? We find the answer in the verse of scripture that immediately precedes this explanation of the hundredfold return. "Then Peter began to say unto him, Lo, we have *left all*, and have followed thee" (Mark 10:28).

Note the words "began to say." In response to Jesus' comments about the difficulty of a rich man entering the Kingdom of God, Peter started to say that the disciples had "left everything" to follow Him. Jesus responded immediately with His famous words about the hundredfold return.

Jesus was explaining that the hundredfold return is available only to those who have "left everything" to follow Him. The hundredfold return is *only* available to those who put Jesus Christ first—ahead of everything else. People who are selfishly claiming worldly possessions as a result of their giving might as well save their breath. They are putting worldly possessions ahead of God and they don't qualify for any hundredfold return! In fact, their selfishness actually *blocks God from* giving to them.

In order to receive the hundred-fold return, we must forsake everything else and follow Jesus Christ. We must put Him ahead of "our" homes, "our" families and "our" possessions and we must keep Him first in every area of our lives. When we do this, Mark 10:30 tells us that we will be "persecuted." The world will criticize our total dedication to Jesus Christ. All of this is part of the price of receiving the hundred-fold return here on this earth.

If we want to qualify for this hundredfold return, do we have to sell our home and automobiles and give the proceeds to God and go off to another country as a missionary? I don't think so. I believe that we have to be *willing* to do any or all of these things and anything else that God's Holy Spirit leads us to do. God knows our hearts and He knows every one of our thoughts (Hebrews 4:13; I Chronicles 28:9). We couldn't fool Him if we wanted to. He knows whether we really have taken the one thing in this world that we have complete control over—our will . . . our power to choose—and willingly surrendered it to Him.

Only Christians who have passed God's scrutiny are eligible to receive a hundredfold return on this earth. Do you qualify? I ask you to take a hard look at yourself and your faith by honestly answering the following questions:

(1) Have I really put the Lord first in every area of my life?

(2) Have I studied His laws of prosperity and am I following these laws?

(3) Do I really want Him to shower financial blessings on me, not for my own selfish desires, but to use these financial blessings to do His will?

If you can honestly answer a definite "yes" to each of these three questions, realize that God is looking for you just as much as you are looking for Him to use you. "For the eyes of the Lord run to and fro throughout the whole earth, to shew himself strong in the behalf of them whose heart is perfect toward him . . ." (II Chronicles 16:9).

In these last days before Jesus comes, our Father wants to raise up an army of His children who will put Him first in every area of their lives and will give freely of their tithes and offerings. He wants this select group to continue to give more and more freely as He gives back to them. He wants this group to give 20%, 30%, 50%, 70% and 90% and even more of its income for His work here on earth. These are the people who will receive the hundredfold return here on this earth and these are the people who will have great treasure when they get to heaven.

Chapter Sixteen

Applying God's Laws of Prosperity

God's laws of prosperity are for us to use now while we're here on earth. "For this commandment which I command thee this day, it is not hidden from thee, neither is it far off. It is not in heaven, that thou shouldest say, Who shall go up for us to heaven, and bring it unto us, that we may hear it and do it?" (Deuteronomy 30:11-12).

We won't need these laws of prosperity in heaven. Everyone will be prosperous there. These laws are very clear. Will you study them? Will you apply these laws during the remainder of your life here on earth?

Many people will say that these laws won't work. In fact, some "religious" people will tell you that these laws won't work. However, our Father in heaven says that they *will* work and ". . . there hath not failed one word of all his good promise . . ." (I Kings 8:56). Every one of the laws of prosperity in this book is based upon instructions from God's Word.

Don't be influenced by people who have never studied and meditated day and night on this subject or stepped out in faith as a result of their study and meditation. Try these laws for yourself.

Pay the price of continual study and meditation. Dare to believe God. Put God's laws of prosperity to the test.

There is only one thing on this earth that can stop God's children from prosperity and that is ourselves! This book contains everything that any of us will ever need in order to be financially success- ful *regardless* of the world's economic condition. It also contains the principles that will enable us to prosper in every other area of our lives.

However, none of these facts will have any lasting effect upon your life unless you take defin- ite, specific steps to actually put these laws to use. If you don't do this now, you'll soon forget this material. Studies have proven conclusively that a message read or heard only once is almost com- pletely forgotten within thirty days. The only way to retain these laws of prosperity is to study them and to meditate on them constantly and then to apply them in our lives.

This isn't easy. It is hard work. God's laws of prosperity won't do you any good until this informa- tion is transferred from these printed pages into your mind and down into your heart and, then, out of your mouth. Then you must act in faith upon these laws.

God's laws of prosperity are spiritual laws. They reach beyond the realm of man's world. They were given to us by the Creator of the entire universe. Diligent study and meditation is required in order to put these laws into effect. In my experiences as a Bible teacher and elder of our church and in counseling with many Christians, I have found that only a very few Christians are willing to pay the price of constant study and meditation that God requires in II Timothy 2:15, Psalm 1:1-4, and Joshua 1:8.

I have laid the foundation by digging out many verses of scripture on God's laws of prosperity, I advise you to go back to the beginning of this book and read it again with pen in hand. Underline material that you wish to retain. Write notes in the margins. Put asterisks (*) next to material that is especially important to you. Write notes in the margins. Draw rectangular blocks around verses of scripture and other material that you want to meditate on.

One of the big differences between studying and reading is that studying requires us to "mark up" the material that we're studying with a pen or a pencil. Look up every verse of scripture in your own Bible and see them with your own eyes in God's Word. Mark them in your Bible by drawing a rectangle, underlining them or marking them with a Bible highlighter.

The next step is to summarize all key points on 3" by 5" cards. Each verse of scripture should be capitalized or underlined so that it stands out. Now you are ready to start meditating on God's laws of prosperity. Follow the procedures that were explained in chapter six. Take one card at a time and carry it with you all day long. Spend a few minutes alone in the morning meditating on the information on that particular card. Turn it over and over in your mind. Think how the scriptural laws on the card apply to your life.

Continue to meditate on this throughout the day. Meditate on this information while you're dressing and washing and brushing your teeth. Perhaps you can place this card on the dashboard of your automobile while you drive to work. Turn this information over and over in your mind throughout the day—when you have a break, on your lunch hour and when you're driving home. Continue in the evening.

While you're meditating on this material throughout the day, open your mouth and speak God's Word with your lips. Do this over and over. I have seen very few Christians who actually open their mouths and continually speak the Word of God. Meditation must include the constant speaking of God's Word. It is an integral part of God's laws of prosperity.

As you go through the process of meditating on these verses of scripture and speaking them with your mouth, go slowly. Don't rush. Wait on the Lord. Turn these great laws over and over in your mind. Do this slowly, thoroughly and thoughtfully.

As this process continues day after day, week after week and month after month, your mind will become more and more renewed to God's laws of prosperity. One at a time, these great laws will drop from your mind into your heart. Soon, your heart will be overflowing with our Father's great truths. They will "explode" deep down inside of you. You'll constantly see new shades of meaning in scripture verses that you thought that you understood completely. You'll constantly come across new levels of awareness of how our Father wants us to live our lives.

Don't ever stop this process of daily meditation. Continue to meditate constantly on God's laws of prosperity and the other great laws in His Word. The more we learn, the more we realize how much there still is to learn. God's laws are infinite. We'll never come close to learning them all. It is overwhelming to even contemplate the sum total of all that is contained in the Bible.

As the process of study and meditation goes on and on, you then must put these laws to work. You need to give cheerfully and freely of yourself and "your" money. Happiness on this earth comes from doing what we know God wants us to do. "If ye *know* these things, *happy* are ye if ye *do* them" (John 13:17).

As we look again at Joshua 1:8—the only verse of scripture that tells us what to do in order to be both prosperous and successful, we again see the three point checklist that tells us that we should, (a) *meditate* day and night in God's Word, (b) *speak* God's Word continually with our mouths and, (c) live our daily lives by actually *doing* everything that God's Word tells us to do. After all of the study and meditation, after speaking God's Word constantly with our mouths, we then must *do* what our Father tells us to do.

It's all here. This book contains everything that you need to know about God's laws of prosperity. I pray fervently that you will be willing to pay the price to learn these laws and apply them in your life. God will bless you abundantly if you do.

What Did You Learn From This Book?

One way of finding out how much you have retained from this book is to take the following test. How many answers do you know now—while this book is still fresh in your mind? I suggest that you mark your calendar to take this test again on a specific date—thirty to ninety days from now, to check your retention after a period of time.

This book will only help you to the degree that it can persuade you to change your habits to line up with the laws of prosperity that our Father has given to us. Check your present habits against the following:

Question	Page Ref.
1. If someone told you that the Bible is full of objections to financial prosperity, how would you answer this question?	14
2. If someone told you that the Bible says that "money is the root of all evil," how would you respond?	14-15
3. The Bible clearly tells us that Abraham enjoyed great financial prosperity. As Christians, how does Abraham's prosperity relate to us?	16
4. If someone told you that God does not want us to be well off financially, what two verses of scripture would you give that person to show that this statement is not true?	16-17

5. How can we explain the abundance that our Father wants us to enjoy by drawing an analogy to seeds inside of fruit? 18

6. Second Corinthians 8:9 tells us that Jesus Christ became poor so that we might be rich. If someone told you that this applies only to spiritual riches and not the financial riches, what would you reply? 19-20

7. Was Jesus Christ really poor financially during His earthly ministry? This book gives several examples to prove that He wasn't. Can you name at least four of these examples? 23-25

8. What are the four words that summarize the difference between God's laws of prosperity and the world's system of prosperity? 28

9. Is God really first in your life? How can you measure this specifically? 29

10. God's Word gives us two definite requirements that we must fulfill if we want to enjoy riches, honor and long life. What are these two requirements? 30

11. If we are in the midst of severe financial problems, it is possible for us to enjoy God's perfect peace in the midst of all of these problems. What are the two scriptural requirements for God's perfect peace? 33

12. The Bible teaches that God's laws of prosperity are based upon the fact that He owns everything and that we own nothing. What verses of scripture explain this to us? 34-35

13. If someone said to you, "God doesn't want us to prosper. The Bible says that it is easier for a camel to go through the eye of a needle than for a rich man to enter into the kingdom of God," how would you answer this? 35-36

153

26. How would you explain the difference between "reading" the Bible and "studying" the Bible?   52-53

27. There is only one verse of scripture in the entire Bible that uses the words "prosperous" and "success" in the same verse. This verse tells us that we must do three things in order to be prosperous and successful. What are they?   54-55

28. Would you like to prosper in every area of your life? The Bible tells us "whatsoever he doeth shall prosper." Exactly what requirements must be met if we are to enjoy this prosperity in every area of our lives?   55-56

29. If a severe economic recession or depression comes upon us, the Bible teaches that one thing above all else will cause problems for Christians. What is this?   56

30. The Bible teaches that one primary requirement for success and prosperity is constant meditation in God's Word. Exactly what does it mean to "meditate" in the Bible?   57-58

31. What is the difference between meditating in the Bible and other forms of meditation such as transcendental meditation and yoga?   58

32. This book explains a specific system of meditation that can be used by any Christian. Exactly how does this system of meditation work?   59-60

33. God's Word tells us that prosperity and hard work go together. Five verses in the Proverbs tells us to compare our work with the work of an ant. What specifically can we learn from observing how an ant works?   64

34. One of the primary causes of the financial problems in our economy today is the large number of workers who expect a full day's

156

come upon us and overtake us. What will cause this to happen? 82-83

46. Many Christians think that they understand God's laws of prosperity, but we all have to pass tests in two specific areas to show what we really know about God's Word. What are these two areas? 83

47. Throughout the Bible we see one continuing law which tells us how to receive. If we want to receive anything, what is the first thing that we must do? 84-86

48. God's Word very definitely tells us that it is possible to be in a position where all of our financial needs will be abundantly supplied and we will also have an abundance left over to give to every good cause that we are led to give to. Exactly what do we need to do in order to get into this desirable financial position? 86-88

49. God is very wealthy. The Bible says that He owns the earth and everything on the earth. If this is so, why is it that His Word places such an emphasis on giving? 89-90

50. People often say, "I'd like to give, but I don't have anything to give." What does God's Word say about this? 91

51. What are the two primary reasons why our Father wants so much for us to prosper financially? 93

52. Would you like to be in a financial position where you are able to give tremendous sums of money to various Christian causes? This definitely is possible. Exactly what do we need to do in order to get into this unique financial position? 95-96

53. God's Word tells us exactly why we should tithe. Why does God want us to tithe? 97

Have You Entered Into the Kingdom of God?

You have just read a complete summary of God's laws of prosperity. These are laws that our Father has written for His children—those human beings who have entered into His kingdom. I ask each reader of this book, "Have *you* entered into the kingdom of God?"

Jesus Christ said, ". . . Verily, verily, I say unto thee, except a man be born again, he cannot see the kingdom of God" (John 3:3). Jesus went on to say, ". . . ye must be born again" (John 3:7). It is very clear that there is only one way to enter into the kingdom of God and that is to be "born again."

We don't enter into God's kingdom by church attendance, by teaching Sunday School, by baptism, by confirmation or by living a good life. Jesus Christ paid the price for every one of us to enter into God's kingdom, but this is not "automatic." Many people are so caught up with their own religious denomination or their own personal beliefs that they completely miss God's specific instructions as to how to enter into His kingdom—for the rest of our lives on earth and also for eternity in heaven.

In order to become a born-again Christian, we first of all, must admit that we are sinners (Romans 3:23, James 2:10). We must admit that there is absolutely no way that we can enter into God's Kingdom based upon our own merits. Next, we have to genuinely repent of our sins (Luke 13:3, Acts 3:19).

After this admission of sin and repentance there is one additional step that must be taken in order to become a born-again Christian. "For if you *tell others* with our own mouth that Jesus Christ is your Lord, and *believe* in your own heart that God has raised Him from the dead, you *will* be saved. For it is by believing in his *heart* that a man becomes right with God; and with his *mouth* he tells others of his faith, confirming his salvation" (Romans 10:9-10 *The Living Bible).*

Many people know that Jesus Christ died for our sins. However, knowledge isn't enough. Intellectual agreement isn't enough. In order to be born again, we have to accept Jesus as our Saviour in our *hearts* and not just in our heads. We're not born again until we come to Him as admitted sinners and trust Him deep down in our hearts as the only way that we can enter into the kingdom of God. God knows exactly what we believe deep down in our hearts (I Samuel 16:7, I Chronicles 28:9, Hebrews 4:13).

We must believe in our hearts that Jesus Christ is the Son of God, that He was born of a virgin, that He died on the cross to pay for our sins, that He rose again from the dead and that He lives today. In order to be a born-again Christian, Romans 10:9-10 tells us that we must not only believe this in our hearts, but we *also* must open our *mouths* and tell

164

others of this belief. This confirms our salvation.

When you believe this in your heart and tell others of this belief with your mouth, *then* you are a born-again Christian. All of us were born naturally on the day that our mothers gave birth to us. We must have a second birth—a spiritual birth—in order to enter into God's Kingdom. "For you have a new life. It was not passed on to you from your parents, for the life they gave you will fade away. This new one will last forever, for it comes from Christ, God's ever-living Message to men" (I Peter 1:23 *The Living Bible*).

God wants us to come to Him, not as intellectuals, but as little children. God doesn't reveal Himself to us through our intellects. He reveals Himself to us through our hearts and, in order to enter into His Kingdom, we must come to Him as little children. We may be adults in the natural world, but in the spiritual world we have to start all over. We have to be born again as spiritual babies. Jesus said, ". . . except ye be converted and become as little children, ye shall not enter into the kingdom of heaven" (Matthew 18:3).

The following prayer will cause you to become born again if you believe this in your heart and open your mouth and tell others of this belief:

"Dear Father, I come to You in the Name of Jesus Christ. I admit that I am a sinner and I know that there is no way that I can enter into Your Kingdom based upon the sinful life that I have led. I'm genuinely sorry for my sins and I ask for Your mercy. I believe in my heart that Jesus Christ is Your Son—that He was born of a virgin, that He died on the cross to pay for my sins, that You raised Him from the dead

165

and that He is alive today. I trust in Him as my only way of entering into Your Kingdom. I confess now to You, Father, that Jesus Christ is my Saviour and my Lord and I will tell others of this decision now and in the future. Thank You, Father. Amen."

When you believe this in your heart and confess this to others with your mouth, you have been reborn spiritually. You are brand new in the spiritual realm. "Therefore if any man be in Christ, he is a *new* creature: old things are *passed away;* behold *all* things have become new" (II Corinthians 5:17).

Now that you have a new, recreated spirit, you are ready to study, understand and obey God's laws of prosperity and all of His other laws. This will transform the rest of your life on earth and you also will live forever in heaven. "For God so loved the world, that he gave his only begotten Son, that whosoever believeth in him should not perish, but have everlasting life" (John 3:16).

A Request to Our Readers

Has this book helped you? If so, would you be willing to tell others so that this book can help them too? Many people are naturally skeptical about the advertising claims for a book such as this. This is why we use a large number of "testimonials" from satisfied readers in our advertising for this book.

If this book has helped you, I'd appreciate it if you would write to me in care of the publisher. Please tell me in your own words how this book has helped you and why you would recommend it to others. Please give us as much information as you can.

Also, we will need your written permission to use any part or all of your comments, your name and the town or city that you live in (we never use street addresses) for our advertising for this book.

Thank you for helping us and, most important, for helping others.

Jack Hartman
Word Associates
P.O. Box 3293
Manchester, NH 03105

Another Book by Jack Hartman

nuggets of faith

Jack Hartman is a self-employed businessman. In 1974, he was on the verge of bankruptcy and a nervous breakdown. He was almost paralyzed by worry and fear. At that time he accepted Jesus Christ as Saviour and Lord.

He immediately started to study and meditate day and night in the Holy Scriptures. From the very first day of this study and meditation the Lord led him to write "Spiritual Meditations" on the spiritual truths that he learned that day. He now has written over 20,000(!) of these meditations and he continues to write them almost every day of his life.

Mr. Hartman now has written a book of his best spiritual meditations on the subject of faith. The title of this book is *Nuggets of Faith*. There are over eighty of these "nuggets" (average length—3 paragraphs) which are the result of thousands of hours of research and study.

There are no wasted words in this book. Each of these "nuggets" goes straight to the point. This book will give you maximum results in a minimum of time. It will make you think.

You can easily read this book in one day. On the other hand, each of these "nuggets" contains enough depth so that you can take one "nugget" with you in the morning and dwell on it throughout the day, turning its scriptural truth over and over in your mind as you meditate on how this scriptural truth can apply to your life.

Nuggets of Faith can be ordered for $2.50 per copy plus 10% postage and handling. The order form for this is at the end of this book.

Cassette Tapes
by Jack Hartman

Tape #	Title

01H   **How To Study The Bible (Part I)**—21 scriptural reasons why it is so important to study the Bible.

02H   **How To Study The Bible (Part II)**—a step-by-step detailed explanation of a proven effective system for studying the Bible (our most demanded tape).

03H   **Enter Into God's Rest**—Don't struggle and strain with loads that are too heavy for you. Learn exactly what God's Word teaches about relaxing under pressure.

04H   **Freedom From Worry**—a comprehensive scriptural explanation on how to become completely free from worry.

05H   **God's Strength—Our Weakness**—God's strength is available to the degree that we can admit our human weakness and trust, instead, in His unlimited strength.

06H   **How To Transform Our Lives**—a thorough, scriptural study of how we can change our lives completely through a complete spiritual renewal of our minds.

07H   **The Greatest Power In The Universe (Part I)**—the greatest power in the universe is love. Part I gives a beautiful scriptural explanation of our Father's love for us.

08H   **The Greatest Power In The Universe (Part II)**—a thorough scriptural explanation on our love for God, our love for each other and overcoming fear through love.

09H   **How Well Do You Know Jesus Christ?**—an Easter Sunday message that received great audience response. After this message, you'll know Jesus Christ as you never knew Him before.

10H   **God's Perfect Peace**—In a world of unrest, people everywhere are searching for inner peace. This is a detailed scriptural explanation of how to obtain God's perfect peace.

11H   **Freedom Through Surrender**—Millions of people are trying to find freedom by "doing their own thing." God's Word tells us to do just the opposite. Freedom comes only as a result of daily surrender of our lives to Jesus Christ.

12H   **Overcoming Anger**—Do you know when anger is permissible and when it is a sin? Learn step-by-step procedures from the Bible on how to overcome the sinful effects of anger.

13H   **Taking Possession Of Our Souls**—God's Word teaches that patience is the key to the possession of our souls. Learn why God allows us to have severe problems, why He sometimes makes us wait for His answer and how to increase patience and endurance.

14H   **Staying Young In The Lord**—Our generation tries to cover up the aging process with makeup, hair coloring, hairpieces, etc. The Bible teaches us a better way. Learn specific factual methods to offset the aging process.

Book and Cassette Tape Order Form

To order books and cassette tapes by Jack Hartman, please use this order form:

Book Or Cassette Tape	# of Copies	Total Price
Trust God For Your Finances ($4.95 ea.)	_____	$_____
Nuggets Of Faith ($2.50 ea.)	_____	$_____

Cassette tapes ($4.00 ea. - $3.00 ea.
if three or more tapes are ordered).

Check the tapes that you wish to order.

___01H ___02H ___03H ___04H ___05H
___06H ___07H ___08H ___09H ___10H
___11H ___12H ___13H ___14H   _____ $_____

Total Price — Books and Tapes $_____
Add 5% Postage and Handling   _____

Enclosed Check or Money Order $_____

Make check payable to: Word Associates
Mail order to: P.O. Box 3293
Manchester, NH 03105

Please print your name and address **clearly**:

Name _____

Address _____

City _____

State or Province _____

Zip or Postal Code _____

Foreign orders must be submitted in U.S. dollars.
Foreign orders are shipped by uninsured surface mail. We ship all orders within 48 hours of receipt of order.
We will give you a full refund on books and cassette tapes if you are dissatisfied in any way.